W0009054

The BIRTHING of a PROPHET

Prophetess VETER NICHOLS

Edited by: Paula R. Bryant, ASarah Publications (www.asarah.com)
Cover design: Ron King, Higher Impact Designs (www.higherimpactdesigns.com)

Copyright © 2003, 2004 by Veter Nichols
ISBN 1-932787-00-3
Library of Congress Control Number: 2004090081

Flow Publications
www.flowpublications.com

To my loving husband, William…

You shared the growth, development, and mentorship of this special
young woman with me. You helped keep us grounded so that
we could fulfill the mandate God had entrusted to us.

To my precious daughters,
Cherise Donyell and Bridgette Camille…

You walked out this journey as well with great passion and love.
You hung in there with us. Thank you both for allowing
Juanita to become your sister and a part of our family.

To my awesome mother, the late Evangelist Margaret Hill…

All I have written is because of you and what you've taught me.
You showed me how important endurance truly is. I first saw the
epitome of real motherhood in you. Your love for humanity
was unending. I will always thank you…for every lesson,
every prayer, every word, and most of all, your great love.

To my beloved godmother, the late Mother Rosie Katherlean Lott…

You were one of my greatest mentors. You loved me as your very own.
You were a pillar of strength for me. You called me your "Proverbs 31"
woman, and I will try to live up to that for as long as I live.
Thank you for sharing your life and family with us.
I was privileged and honored to have known you.

To Elder Thomas and Mother Katherine Bynum…

I truly thank you for including my husband and me in your
daughter's life. Thank you for sharing her with us.

To my spiritual daughter, Myama "Mya" Boone…

May God bless you for all of your time, help, and expertise
in the writing of this book. I pray that you complete
everything He has put in your heart.

And last, but certainly not least,
to my spiritual first born, Juanita Bynum.

Without you, this book would not exist. Thank you for giving us the
freedom to speak into your life without reservation. You are a shining
example of what birthing a spiritual lineage is all about. If you hadn't
gotten off the train that day and made the choice to be and stay broken,
the world may never have known the woman of God you have become.
What a blessing it has been to see you lay down your life for the
sake of the "call"…you are truly an appointed prophet in this hour.

Table of Contents

Foreword

Dr. Juanita Bynum Weeks

A strong spiritual mother is a precious gift. Like a natural mother, she loves unconditionally and is willing to endure great pain to deliver a healthy baby into the world. She sees with the eyes of the Spirit—beyond failures, broken promises, and every kind of messy situation to give birth to divine destiny.

I am truly thankful for the powerful women that God, in His sovereignty, placed in my life. Among them are two special people who birthed out the prophet in me: my mother, Katherine Bynum, and Veter Nichols (my Pastor's wife in Port Huron, Michigan), a powerful prophetess and spiritual mother. I don't know where I would be today if God hadn't used these strong women to mentor me and shape my character.

God brought Prophetess Nichols into my life when my ministry was young and everything I had tried to do on my own was falling apart. Feeling ashamed and isolated, I tried to handle my problems without any help, *but I couldn't*. And I lost it. Several times.

Whenever I think about that midnight season when I was crawling out of "the sheets," I shout praises to God for allowing her entry into my brokenness. In fact, God used both Prophetess and Pastor Nichols to embrace my pain, and as a result, they helped to release my potential. With the love and understanding only true spiritual parents can give, they reached down to help me...and I rose up from the ashes into my divine calling and destiny.

Oh, yes! The enemy tried to abort me before God's purpose could be birthed in my spirit—*but God had already provided a way of escape.* He planted a tiny seed in the spiritual womb of a willing servant: someone that would obey Him and labor with me until my appointed time of delivery. Let me pause here and say, "Prophetess Nichols, I can't thank you enough for all of the wisdom, prayers, tears, and love you sowed into my life. You took a death walk with me...I am eternally grateful."

Hear me. This is more than a story about what God birthed through the mutual struggle of two women. It's a call to spiritual parents everywhere. The season of birthing is here! It's time for spiritual mothers to rise up and embrace the call to birth out many babies in the Spirit realm. The prophetic ministry, among many others, depends on it. As a prophet, let me exhort you—*prophets must be nurtured, developed, and released to declare His words in this final hour.* Don't be disobedient if the Lord plants a seed in your spiritual womb. You never know whose destiny will be released when you say, "Yes" to God.

On the other hand, you may be that prophetic seed. You may be going through what seems to be the worst time of your life. If so, you're taking a death walk like I did. Listen to me. Make sure you have a spiritual mother (*and* father) to whom you can be accountable. Get anything out of the way—*especially your pride*—that keeps you from embracing the love and guidance of a true, godly mentor. Don't let depression, shame, or anything else abort God's purposes in your life.

No matter what your story may be, I urge you to receive the words of this anointed vessel of God. And I pray that as you read our story, the truth will set you free.

The Call of the Prophet

Before I formed thee in the belly I knew thee; and
before thou camest forth out of the womb I sanctified thee,
and I ordained thee a prophet unto the nations.
—Jeremiah 1:5

The voice of the Lord speaks to the prophet...choosing him for the call well before birth.

Behold, I have refined thee, but not with silver; **I have chosen thee in the furnace of affliction**.
—Isaiah 48:10 (emphasis mine)

The call of the prophet takes place in the furnace of affliction... his or her reality is deeply embedded in this refining process. Though it may seem difficult, every true prophet must be formed in the fire. God must purify and prove His anointed vessels, for He is raising them up to become His mouthpieces that declare where He is taking the Church. So the fire is vital.

Whenever a transition is about to take place in the body of Christ, God speaks to His prophets, letting them know that changes are coming. These changes can be related to church government (see Acts 13:1–3 and 15:13–21) and/or the individual vision of a man or woman of God (see Acts 9:10–22). This is why a prophet must be tested. An immature and unproven vessel cannot hear God clearly, or be able to boldly declare His words in the earth. The prophet must endure a deep purging so the weight of God's words isn't diminished.

Prophets are raised up to prepare the way and break ground in the Spirit. Within the prophetic lies the powerful root, which I call the *breaker's anointing.* God uses this prophetic anointing to prepare the way for His apostles to establish what has been spoken. Throughout history, God has used prophets when His people were at a major crossroads, such as in Genesis 6–9 when He used Noah to warn his generation about the coming flood. Where there is spiritual blindness, prophets are absolutely necessary—because there is no vision or revelation in the Spirit realm.

> Where there is no vision [no redemptive revelation of God], the people perish…
> —*Proverbs 29:18 AMPL*

Without prophetic voice and vision, people cannot receive and move into the next manifestation of God. And because prophets have an ear to the mouth of God (like Abraham, Moses, Samuel, and others…most importantly, His Son, Jesus) they must clearly utter His voice, or the truth of God cannot be revealed. Therefore, prophets must be sensitized to the Lord so they will be able to reveal His timing, seasons, and divine strategies—declare the next steps that must be taken to advance His Kingdom. Prophets illuminate to others what God desires, because without revelation or direction people have the propensity to cast off all restraints and follow their own fleshly desires. Inevitably, this forfeits God's will and purpose for their lives.

The prophet is often perceived as complex and off-balance. In the natural, these qualities are seen as weaknesses…yet they are common traits of a true prophet. He or she hears and speaks things from God that seem uncustomary or difficult to accept, which often leaves the prophet in a place of solitude and skepticism. Prophets are usually misunderstood because they have a deep understanding of God (birthed from the fires of affliction), Whose wisdom is far above our own. So the words they receive and give (while not necessarily easy) prove to be infinite truth.

In our day and age, God has used women as a prophetic voice alongside of men. Women such as Kathryn Kuhlman, Mary Etta Woodard, and Aimee Simple McPherson have been effectively used by God to minister as His oracles. And, yes, just as He used women in scripture—Deborah, Esther, Isaiah's wife, the woman at the well (John 4:3–42), Mary Magdalene, the daughters of Philip (Acts 21:8–9), and so on—He's still bringing them to the forefront in the twenty-first century. God is still calling and equipping women to be used as powerful voices to the nations.

Another characteristic of prophets is they have an innate ability to "father" and "mother" a people. Oftentimes, their parenting (mentoring) seems harsh and brash, but you must understand, that's the way God has built their character. He knew they would have to speak to a hard-hearted, rebellious people (since we are shaped in iniquity, according to Psalm 51:5); therefore, they would often be required to deliver a hard word. God knew His prophets would have to have a certain depth and strength of character in order to deal with the rejection and dejectedness that come with the call. This is why He can use them to help "shape" others.

True prophets speak God's word exactly as they hear it from the mouth of the Lord, not mincing His words in the least. They do not operate from a selective, compromising position; yet they must use wisdom regarding when to deliver the word. Godly wisdom is an essential part of the prophet's ministry, because if a good word is delivered out of season, it can bring destruction instead of life and prosperity.

This takes me back to sensitivity, because prophets not only hear what God is saying, many times they are capable of feeling the heart of God (as He allows). For instance, if God is grieved with a certain situation, the prophet will also be grieved (which explains why his or her emotions can appear to be off-balance). Prophets constantly change under the burden of the Lord as they receive His message. This literally puts them in the position of delivering the word *exactly* as God has revealed it to their heart and soul.

"Telling it like it is" is unpopular, and like I said before, this often puts the prophet in a lonely position and/or lifestyle. He or she is generally misunderstood. However, when people truly accept God's prophets, He releases blessings of prosperity into their lives (see 2 Chronicles 20:20 and Matthew 10:41). Yes, when they begin to recognize God's voice and hand through His anointed vessels, they come under the supernatural blessing of the Lord.

Elijah is a prime example. He was known as "the troubled prophet." He not only experienced rejection, but also suffered from depression. In times of intense spiritual pressure, Elijah was even known to run.

> But he himself went a day's journey into the wilderness, and came and sat down under a juniper tree: and he requested for himself that he might die; and said, It is enough; now, O LORD, take away my life; for I *am* not better than my fathers.
> —*1 Kings 19:4*

So you see, if you're called to be a prophet, you have to be strong enough to endure backlash, rejection, persecution, and even death...or you'll run when the pressure of the call becomes too intense. Like Elijah, many prophets either suffer from depression, or have sometimes entertained thoughts of suicide, because the call is so heavy. The flesh becomes weak under the "weightiness" of the call.

Being complex and off-balance, a prophet often feels that running is the only recourse...until God sends him an Elisha—someone who will care for and love him unconditionally. One thing is certain with prophets: When they finally slow down and become still, they can hear the voice of the Lord clearly. And when the "fullness of time" comes in any situation, prophets have an innate ability to "switch gears" because timing is vitally important in their lives. A prophet's reality hinges on being sensitive to times and seasons in the Spirit realm.

Yet another aspect of true prophets is they are totally committed to obedience, no matter what they are going through. Let's say you are a prophet. Then you probably have experienced in God that you can be a tremendous blessing to others even when you are going through your own personal "hell." That's why prophets have to be tried in the furnace of affliction. They are required to live on the edge, enduring stress at its highest peak and in seasons where relentless, violent storms seem to rage continually. (As crazy as it may sound, these are actually the best times in the life of a prophet.) Adversity pushes a prophet into his or her destiny at just the right time.

Obviously, there is an appointed time for a prophet to be released into ministry, but this depends on what he or she has learned in the midst of formation. So a prophet must take advantage of "seasons of adversity" in order to embrace the purpose of being broken, transformed, and reformed. That which has been "shaped in iniquity" must learn to say what David prayed unto God, "Purge me with hyssop, and I shall be clean: wash me, and I shall be whiter than snow" (Psalm 51:7).

This is where a mentor comes in. He or she paces the protégé so that the prophet-in-the-making will not miss the blessings to be gained during adverse times—thus bringing soberness and stability, and helping the protégé to stay focused on hearing the wisdom of God. So if you have received the call to be a spiritual parent and mentor, stand strong and be encouraged. This process is necessary. It's how your spiritual son or daughter will learn to convey God's wisdom "in season," when it's vital to the hearer.

On the other hand, if you believe that you're called to the office of a prophet (not just a prophetic anointing), you must *know* this for sure (and not just go by what you feel)—because you must take a death walk. Of all the five-fold ministry gifts, the prophetic office is one of the most difficult to walk out. So you must weigh every detail of this walk to determine if God has really called you to this office—because once you are birthed through your mentor's "spiritual womb," you'll begin the death walk...and there's no turning back.

Still, the office of the prophet certainly has its rewards. Scripture tells us this reward is prosperity, even for those who serve and walk with the prophet (2 Chronicles 20:20, 2 Kings 2:9)

As one who is often referred to as an "Elijah" to an "Elisha," I cannot say the birthing of a prophet is a role that leaves something to be desired. As a spiritual parent alongside of my husband, I often reminisce about the many sons and daughters that have passed through our lives. And now, I realize the great value and impact we have made in the lives of these prophets. We often wonder, *Why us? What have we done that's so special?* (In a way, I'm glad that we can't fully grasp it in this earthly realm.) What I do see and believe that makes us different (and perhaps special in the eyes of others) is we are down-to-earth people who only want the will of God for those He brings into our lives. And no matter how difficult the storm has been, we've always been ready to receive another "spiritual baby."

We also share the burden that prophets need to be better understood so they can function to the fullness of their potential in God. They must fulfill exactly what has been ordained for their lives, for the sake of God's harvest and for His kingdom. I trust the body of Christ will begin to accept the prophets God is raising up in this hour, whether they are male or female—because they truly have an ear to the mouth of God, to hear on our behalf.

As a spiritual mother, I pray that God will raise up more mentors—true spiritual parents—who will be willing to give their lives for the sake of birthing out a prophet in this final hour. I pray that as I take you through my first spiritual pregnancy, you'll gain insight and understanding of the prophet's journey through the birthing process. I pray you'll see how intense it is for a prophet to develop in the womb of the Spirit and ultimately emerge from the birth canal to impact the nations.

Make sure you have a journal and pen handy to answer the questions at the end of each chapter. Because whether you're the "prophet-in-the-making" or the spiritual parent, you're about to embark upon a new journey in God. As you go, I pray for the completion of His purpose in your life. And even more, that your prophetic destiny would be birthed into the earth.

The Gestational Season

of

A Prophet

1

Formed in the Womb

For You did form my inward parts; You did knit
me together in my mother's womb.
—*Psalm 139:13* AMPL

The First Trimester: Weeks 1–12

There were many aspects of Juanita's development, but I want to start by focusing on the inward, spiritual process. In other words, I'm starting where life begins...in the womb. Then we'll move into some of the things we encountered while walking out the stages of her development.

During the first weeks of my "spiritual pregnancy," I became more and more aware of the fetus growing in my "womb." The effects of her presence were sure. I was definitely experiencing something like morning sickness. For most women in the natural realm, the nausea and vomiting often associated with morning sickness wanes after the first few weeks. For me, it took longer.

> **I was shocked....my spiritual womb was behaving just like the physical uterus of a pregnant woman.**

I felt tired. My body was working overtime to create a haven for this new "baby" to form. Honestly, I was shocked. This was my first spiritual pregnancy and my spiritual womb was behaving just like the physical uterus of a pregnant woman. I remembered the first stages of my natural pregnancies...how my uterus became engorged with nutrient-rich blood and expanded to support the life of each of my babies. What a miracle. Because of new life, my body was generating more blood, which traveled through my heart to each unborn child. Closing my eyes and thinking of those precious times, I became aware of a familiar sensation…my spiritual heart rate was picking up.

Spiritually, the nutrient-rich Blood of Christ became the life-giving source to my baby. Through His Blood, she received the Word (i.e., food), protection, and other essential elements for living in the Spirit realm. The Blood also "expanded" and "stretched me out" so that I would have room in my life to carry her to the next level.

> Enlarge the place of thy tent, and let them stretch forth the curtains of thine habitations: spare not, lengthen thy cords, and strengthen thy stakes; For thou shalt break forth on the right hand and on the left; and thy seed shall inherit the Gentiles, and make the desolate cities to be inhabited.
> —*Isaiah 54:2–3*

My heart started beating with even greater intensity and desire as my "spiritual daughter" began to rely more heavily upon me. I knew my family life would change and that everything we'd grown accustomed to would suddenly be different. Pregnancy changed everything. I knew that I would need adequate prenatal care for spiritual support. So I had to stay in a constant state of prayer, communing with the Great Physician during "prenatal check-ups."

The Second Trimester: Weeks 13–27

My first trimester passed and, praise God, I no longer had morning sickness. However, this was still a "high risk" pregnancy. The threat of miscarriage was real. I was still very much in the adjustment process. As time passed, the baby's demands on my body began to cause aches and pains I wasn't sure I wanted to handle. That's when I considered "abortion"—but it was too late. I had to carry my spiritual child full term.

Something unexpected was happening that was different from my natural pregnancies. I remembered feeling my best during the second trimester. Most of the

> **Something unexpected was happening...I felt extremely uncomfortable.**

initial discomforts had passed and the aches and pains of the final trimester were a couple of months away. This time, however, as our "daughter" began to grow—and the muscles and ligaments that supported my "uterus" began to stretch—I felt extremely uncomfortable. I also had a hard time sleeping, because our spiritual baby sometimes kept me up at night with her own personal growth issues.

Juanita continued to develop, and I steadily gained the needed "weight" in the Spirit to support both of our lives. Then suddenly, I began to feel back strain...pressure that resulted from ministering to her needs, and in some ways, neglecting my own. I needed the Great Physician more than ever. As I relied more and more upon Him, the Lord showed me how to lessen the discomforts that were inevitable. In other words, I had to spend more time waiting upon the Lord (see Isaiah 40:27–31). I had to exercise the Word, lift my concerns and petitions to Him in prayer, and learn (in all of the changes that were taking place around me) to rest in His embrace. Jesus was so faithful. He helped me to work through my pregnancy issues, and at the same time, met every need of the "daughter" that would soon come forth.

> God that made the world and all things therein, seeing that he is Lord of heaven and earth, dwelleth not in temples made with

hands; neither is worshipped with men's hands, as though he needed any thing, seeing he giveth to all life, and breath, and all things; and hath made of one blood all nations of men for to dwell on all the face of the earth, and hath determined the times before appointed, and the bounds of their habitation; that they should seek the Lord, if haply they might feel after him, and find him, though he be not far from every one of us: For in him we live, and move, and have our being; as certain also of your own poets have said, For we are also his offspring.
—*Acts 17:24–28*

In the natural, a baby starts moving for the first time between weeks sixteen and twenty. In medical terms, this thrilling event is called *quickening*. Likewise, our daughter was "quickened" in the Holy Spirit during this time. She started learning how to *live, move, and have her being* in God. Her "movements in the Spirit" signified that she was a true prophetess-in-the-making. She began to move forward and make her effect known. Yes, her development in my spiritual womb was becoming apparent.

> **Several tests are administered for high-risk pregnancies...God does the same thing in the Spirit realm.**

My prenatal care also stepped up during this season. It included testing her health and proving her viability and growth, according to 1 Thessalonians 5:21, "Prove all things; hold fast that which is good." Testing was inevitable. She had to know where she was, versus where she should be, in her spiritual development. I had to check her character so that she could discover her resilience in the things of God. Would she develop the ability to withstand the persecution, changes, and storms that would come her way as she came forth from the womb? I had to be certain.

This reminded me of several tests that are administered for high-risk pregnancies. They are designed to either identify or rule out any problems, defects, or disorders in a child's genetic make-up. God does the same thing in the Spirit realm. He tries each person's heart and proves his or her development. Here are a few of the "natural" prenatal tests:

1) The Ultrasound is a routine test that's performed on all expectant mothers. (It uses sound waves to create an internal picture of the developing baby. During this process, the medical caregiver can pinpoint the age of the fetus, detect multiple embryos, and spot conditions such as neural tube defects.)

2) The Alpha-fetoprotein test is useful in the prenatal diagnosis of multiple births or birth defects (that could affect physical, emotional, and/or mental development).

3) The Amniocentesis test is generally offered to women who have an increased risk of birthing a baby with genetic disorders. (During this procedure, a needle is inserted through the abdomen into the amniotic sac to withdraw amniotic fluid. Then cells directly from the fetus are tested for chromosomal defects.)

4) The Glucose Tolerance (i.e., blood sugar) test identifies whether or not a pregnant woman has gestational diabetes.

5) The Hemoglobin test measures the amount of red blood cells in the blood. (Too few blood cells indicates anemia.)

Now let's look at these tests in the Spirit. The "Ultrasound" revealed to us who "our child" was in her fetal stages, while she was in the early stages of divine construction. God created a "picture" of her in the womb, and from seeing this picture, it revealed to us who she would be at the end of the process.

The "Alpha-fetoprotein test" sought out any missing parts in her spiritual development. As a result, God restored some of the things Satan desired to steal during this period. This spiritual test revealed our daughter was under-developed in some chromosomal areas, which means that as God began to "divide" areas of her life, the nucleus of who she was in the Spirit needed to be reinforced. Yet, again, God was faithful. In His grace and mercy, He healed and filled what had been missing and defective.

Due to the high-risk nature of this pregnancy, and the genetic disorders that have historically hindered the development of prophets, the Great Physician had to administer an Amniocentesis. This was extremely uncomfortable for us both. In other words, God had to prick me in order to test her. That's when I discovered areas where I had been in the way. It hurt me to require that Juanita go through this test, but we all knew it was for her greater good.

Two final spiritual tests were administered directly to me, Glucose Tolerance and Hemoglobin. These tests had to make sure the Blood of Christ was serving its purpose. I had to let it wash and cleanse us in purity. I couldn't let anything contaminate the process—because only the Blood was powerful enough to sustain both her life and mine. (Let me say, the Blood of Christ has always been, and will always be, filled with supernatural power! My tests revealed whether I would let His Blood flow freely through every part of my being so that Juanita could receive an untainted anointing.)

It was during this trimester that Juanita's presence in our lives quadrupled in size and effect. She began hearing and responding to sounds in the Spirit, and slowly but surely, God started regulating every area of her life. It took time for her to grow and come into the understanding of who she was destined to become in Christ. And like a natural pregnancy, she became more active as time progressed. I felt each one of her kicks, nudges, and jabs.

The Third Trimester: 28 Weeks to Birth
The third trimester starts the twenty-eighth week of pregnancy, which ends in labor and delivery. Once again, I discovered that many natural and spiritual events during this stage of prenatal development are strikingly similar. In fact, they are mirror images. The natural reflects the supernatural as new changes take place.

Bear in mind, though, times of growth and change in the Spirit differ in every pregnancy, so the "natural" span of each one has little relevance. In the Spirit realm, every "pregnancy" is unique. As a result, the labor and delivery process can be quick, or it could take a number of years (as it was in the case of Elisha the prophet, the spiritual son of Elijah).

> **Every pregnancy is unique...the labor and delivery process can be quick, or it could take a number of years.**

A healthy delivery means the "prophet-in-the-making" has come forth *on time.* In other words, he or she has emerged in ministry according to God's timetable. Even still, sometimes during this season of birthing (though the pregnancy may no longer be considered high risk), unforeseen complications can arise...as you'll see later on. Our spiritual daughter was definitely coming forth, yet at the same time, many questions were raised about God's timing and His workings. We had to *prove all things*, no matter how we interpreted what God was doing in Juanita's life.

We are more convinced today than ever that our daughter's nine-year journey with us in Port Huron, Michigan was all part of her divine destiny. It proved to be her "Samaria"—a place where she would come face-to-face with God. At the time, no one had any idea this would be a "breaking forth" for her—and also the place where she would die. Port Huron was truly the birthplace of her spiritual destiny...where her ministry began.

In some ways, I think of it as the "belly of the whale," where Juanita endured her "Jonah experience" (i.e., a prophet in the Old Testament who learned obedience and the depths of God's infinite mercy while trapped inside of a whale—see the book of Jonah). In other words, the woman that *used to be* came to Port Huron to die and be reformed into the woman of *God's desire.* Juanita wasn't supposed to become the typical speaker or customary C.O.G.I.C. evangelist. Destiny proclaimed that she would be birthed into a great, sovereign call.

During the gestational period, my husband had spoken this into her life. Juanita couldn't become "typical." Her development had been supernatural, so her birthing had to be significant. She had to remain "atypical." Now, many seasons and years later, she has indeed become what had been ordained of God before the foundation of the world. She has literally been transformed into *that* woman, our daughter, and our spiritual lineage...

> **Juanita couldn't become "typical." Her birthing had to be significant.**

Prophetess Dr. Juanita Bynum Weeks

Reflection and Study

1) Has God placed a prophet-in-the-making in your care? If so, how do you know for sure? Can you identify which spiritual trimester you're in?

2) Describe a few of your "morning sickness" symptoms… which areas of your life need to come into balance with what God is doing? Have you sought Godly counsel from your church leadership? What has to change in order for you to be able to carry this spiritual baby?

3) How are you dealing with the "stretching" process described in Isaiah 54? Which areas of your life are being "enlarged" by God? How is it "making room" for your new child in the Spirit?

4) Is your family part of this process? Do they understand this calling of God upon your life? List a few things you can do to help them understand and become part of the birthing process.

5) Are you staying in the Word and spending time in prayer every day to sustain your life and that of your spiritual son or daughter? If not, how can you adjust your schedule to make this your first priority?

6) Have you ever become discouraged and considered having a spiritual abortion? What do you need to do in order to get back on track and carry your baby full term?

7) Is your spiritual pregnancy "high risk"? If so, which of the five tests has God already administered in your life? What were the results? If any issues or defects were revealed, have you allowed God to direct you in correcting them? How?

To the Prophet-in-the-Making

If you are called to be a prophet, how is God "forming" you in the womb? Do you have an open, honest relationship with your spiritual parents? Are you submitted to their leadership and guidance

Read Isaiah 40:3–41:2

2

Spiritual Conception

Before I formed thee in the belly I knew thee…
—Jeremiah 1:5

That Sunday morning in November seemed like any other…until I received the phone call. It was my husband. Earlier that morning, he and our two daughters, Cherise and Bridgette, had left for Sunday school. Now, he was urging me to get to the church as soon as I could—there was someone he wanted me to meet. I sped up my pace and rushed out to church.

As I entered my husband's office, I immediately noticed the beautiful, ebony-skinned young woman with dark, vibrant eyes. There was a hint of mystery beneath her soft smile, yet she had a fiery spark in her eyes that piqued my curiosity. I instantly wanted to know more about her. When we reached out to embrace, I felt as if I already knew her. Little did I know, at that moment, I had

> **I immediately noticed the beautiful, ebony-skinned young woman with dark, vibrant eyes….I felt as if I already knew her.**

embraced destiny—because that November morning, God impregnated me with the "seed" that I'd give birth to nine years later.

The moment I touched her, I sensed a deep bonding and connection. I also discerned that she was indeed special to God. My husband recognized it, as well.

After the meeting, we proceeded with service as usual...and of course, God truly moved. Our ministry, New Hope Tabernacle Church of God in Christ, wasn't your typical C.O.G.I.C. church! During that time, it was highly unusual for a predominantly African-American congregation to have praise and worship active in our services. In reality, we had already been in this vein for a couple of years. And it was clear this was new to the young woman, even though she seemed to enjoy this experience in worship. As we were nearing the end of the service, my husband felt impressed to have her share a testimony...and I can only say, she "tore up" the church!

> **The mystery of who she was in the Spirit started to become apparent.**

As she spoke, the mystery of who she was in the Spirit started to become apparent. We could see the anointing of God was clearly upon her life, so of course, we asked her to come back and minister in the evening service. We were thoroughly impressed. We definitely felt led to receive the ministry of this unique young woman named Juanita.

That night, she preached a message entitled, "Bear Down and Push Out." Thinking about it later, I realized how ironic it was that her first opportunity to bring a word would be a prophetic insight into the relationship God wanted us to have with her. God deposited Juanita into our lives at the same time that she preached a message about the concept of "birthing." At the time, we didn't realize we'd endure this process with Juanita—our meeting was to be the beginning of an intense spiritual journey.

The word Juanita gave was definitely for our church, but more importantly, *it was for her*. It was a self-prophecy of sorts that would soon be revealed. Now we realize the word was even more than that. God meant for it to help the church learn how to relate to the position she'd eventually have.

Juanita returned two weeks later as our guest speaker for a five-day revival. Again, it was a powerful move of God. We experienced healing, deliverance, and breakthrough in our ministry. Souls were saved and set free. We were truly blessed. Yet, there was something missing…

After such a remarkable outpouring of God's power, we never would have dreamed there were many things in her life that still needed to be healed. How could it be possible for God to use her like that if she wasn't "ready" for ministry? From experiencing the powerful anointing on her life, it *appeared* Juanita was already on her way. She possessed an awesome ability to

> **Everything was in place, or so it seemed. Soon, I discovered what was missing…**

speak into the lives of God's people. It was more than apparent. Everything was in place, or so it seemed. Soon, I discovered what was missing. Juanita definitely had the gifts and anointing of a prophetess, but she lacked character.

According to Romans 11:29, "…the gifts and calling of God *are* without repentance." As we moved into the birthing process, this helped me to understand why she was able to operate so powerfully in our services. Added to this, Juanita used her prophetic gift and call to bless God's people. And most importantly, God is sovereign. He loves His people, so He used Juanita in spite of herself, because she availed herself to be used. Let me pause here and say: God doesn't want to use us in this way. First, He wants us to become ambassadors of Christ. As such, our lives should be a testimony of His character.

Juanita was already a prophetess, because she was born for it. But when the "forming" process began, she had to go back to the beginning…to be shaped, molded, and made to become who God intended her to be before the foundation of the world. In other words, Juanita had to die so that her true identity in Christ could be resurrected from the ashes of her death to self-will.

> **Juanita had to die so that her true identity in Christ could be resurrected.**

It was apparent that God wanted her to be a part of our lives. Yet what seemed like it should have been an easy growth process (in my spiritual womb) developed into a nine-year pregnancy. I quickly learned that the gestational season of a prophet can be very rigorous—but as it was with Juanita, it's quite another matter to endure this process when the child is fully developed.

Slowly, I began to realize it was going to be a difficult pregnancy. Juanita was going to be an extremely active "baby"—in other words, not easily contained. Little did I know that I'd face the threat of spiritual miscarriage many times. God would have to "enlarge" me for the life already growing within my spiritual womb.

Our First Trimester Begins

Juanita had traveled a long way to be birthed out in the Spirit. At the time, her life and home were in Chicago, Illinois, where she was living with her new husband. So we strongly encouraged them to move to Port Huron. They agreed to relocate, and moved within two weeks.

> **When Juanita got off the train, God immediately gave me a vision.**

When Juanita got off the train, God immediately gave me a vision. He opened her life before me like a book; I became a witness to the hurt, pain, rejection, mental struggles, and abuse she had suffered. This vision confirmed to me that I was indeed pregnant with this young woman's destiny. Initially, I only had a sense of connection, yet the moment she got off the train, God verified the reality that I was pregnant with a new "baby." So I began the process of getting to know Juanita, sensing and experiencing her in every way on a spiritual level.

God enhanced my view of her life by performing a spiritual "Ultrasound" (of sorts) about a week after she and her husband moved into our home. Juanita and I were in the kitchen. She was getting ready to style my hair...and as soon as she touched my head, I saw an incident that had occurred in her life. *It was as clear as day.* I turned around in my chair and our eyes met. As I gave a detailed description of all that I'd seen, Juanita began to weep so profusely that her legs buckled! Then she fell to her knees, crying, and laid her head in my lap.

She began sharing intimate stories from her life. At that moment, the reality of who she was meant to be in my life became "clear." That's also when I believe she began to accept me as her "spiritual mother," because that's when she began to trust the anointing of God *in me*...

> There remaineth therefore a rest to the people of God. For he that is entered into his rest, he also hath ceased from his own works, as God *did* from his. Let us labour therefore to enter into that rest, lest any man fall after the same example of unbelief. For the word of God *is* quick, and powerful, and sharper than any twoedged sword, piercing even to the dividing asunder of soul and spirit, and of the joints and marrow, and *is* a discerner of the thoughts and intents of the heart. Neither is there any creature that is not manifest in his sight: but all things *are* naked and opened unto the eyes of him with whom we have to do.
> —*Hebrews 4:9–13*

Soon, we all became one spiritual family. Juanita called my husband and me *Dad* and *Mom*, and Cherise and Bridgette became her sisters. We had entered into what God had ordained from before the foundation of the world. Juanita was truly becoming our daughter; *it was real*. Today, nearly twenty-five years later, we love her as much as ever.

> **Juanita was truly becoming our daughter...it was real.**

On that day of revelation and discovery, Juanita's end met her beginning. The true prophetess within was preparing to come forth from the ashes of her past. Yes, it was time for her to be "formed in the womb."

After the unveiling, the first thing my husband did was to take her engagement book, which contained pastor's names for all of her speaking engagements. He said to her, "You aren't going to be like every other evangelist, preaching with no character or integrity. We see greatness in you!"

As we were seeking how to develop that greatness, I heard the voice of God tell me to go to the Christian bookstore and purchase a book entitled, *Daughter of Destiny: the Life of Kathryn Kuhlman*. As I obeyed, I was startled that our own spiritual daughter would live a life reminiscent of such a powerful woman of God. Then in the Spirit, I saw Juanita come out of obscurity to preach at a large Church of God in Christ convention— and she was speaking before a massive audience. (This actually came to pass in May 2002, when she spoke at the International Women's Convention of the Church of God in Christ.)

> **God showed me that she would rise out of obscurity to become one of the most influential women in ministry.**

God showed me, before anyone had ever heard of "Juanita Bynum," that she would rise out of obscurity to become one of the most influential women in ministry—and not just in the African-American church; in the body of Christ, worldwide. She would come from meager beginnings and grow into a prosperous woman...a true daughter of destiny.

In the "belly" of her making, there would indeed be pain, trial, and labor. And as her spiritual mother and mentor, I felt her difficult beginnings. Finally, after getting to know the depths of her testimony, "hell" began breaking loose. Morning sickness invaded me every day and night.

As I said before, Juanita and her husband had moved in with our family, so my husband and I wanted to help them keep their new marriage strong. We started counseling them, even though we weren't sure if their marriage would last...*because there was so much deception*. Their union was rocky, to say the least, yet they tried to make it work for nearly two years. Both were gifted musically and prophetically. They could sing, preach, and prophesy. Yet, as a couple, they couldn't get along.

Juanita loved her husband with all her heart and virtually carried the marriage, because she desperately wanted it to succeed. At times, she even worked three jobs to support them financially and still took care of things at home. Between jobs, she also styled hair to supplement their income. However, her husband was negligent in his duties, which caused tension, anger, and bitterness between them. It was apparent that one person giving *two hundred percent* in the marriage couldn't compensate for two people giving *one hundred percent each* to make it work. As much as Juanita tried to make their marriage successful, she ultimately paid the heavier price.

My husband and I recognized they were both too young and immature for marriage. Juanita's husband made decisions she didn't agree with...even down to the company he chose to keep. And he refused to change or reverse his decisions. This hurt her deeply, and in time, it killed the marriage.

Eventually, "dad" had to advise Juanita that if her husband decided to leave, she should let him go. In fact, he even prophesied that this young man would leave. These words rang true on her husband's birthday.

I still remember it vividly. Juanita was excited about giving him the gift she had bought for his birthday. So when he came to her job, she was certain it was just to see her and to get the gift. Instead, she soon learned he'd come to tell her that he was leaving...the marriage was over. He'd already packed his things (in the car she'd bought with her hard-earned money), and told her that he'd only stopped by as a "courtesy." Needless to say, she didn't give him the radio (his birthday gift). Instead, she gave it to my husband.

> **We watched her suffer...and yet remain faithful, despite carrying the tremendous burden of a broken heart.**

The marital stress and strain took its toll on her body. Consequently, Juanita endured the heartache of three miscarriages—right in our home. Over time, we watched her suffer through the marriage and yet remain faithful despite carrying the tremendous burden of a broken heart. We knew that even though it would be extremely painful, her husband had to leave so she could be free. *Don't get me wrong*, we're not anti-marriage; but this was a union of the flesh. Clearly, Juanita had not truly consulted God. Yet He was merciful to make a way for her to be released from this bondage in accordance with His Word.

Then there was the courtroom experience...Juanita was absolutely miserable. It nearly killed her emotionally to stand before a judge and obtain a divorce decree. She was broken and dying throughout the entire proceedings. And at the end of the matter, *a part of Juanita was gone.*

Losing the man she loved left a void inside of her heart, so subconsciously, she started doing everything she could to fill it. She began going from one relationship with a man to another. It hurt us deeply to watch our "baby" go through these "withdrawals" and cycles of pain. Juanita made one bad decision after another—and ultimately hurt herself the most. Trying desperately to heal her broken heart...she used every remedy to stop the pain...but nothing erased or removed it. Her self-prescribed "medications" only made matters worse.

Reflection and Study

1) Where and how did you meet your spiritual son or daughter? Describe what happened in your spirit when you met this prophet-in-the-making.

2) Did you discern immediately what your role would be in his or her life? Why? Why not?

3) What has God revealed to you about your spiritual child's ministry? What is he or she called and anointed to do in the kingdom?

4) Do you discern a balance of gifts and character in your spiritual child, or is something out of balance? What steps has God given you to address it?

5) Have you experienced a "day of revelation and discovery," like Juanita and I did in the kitchen that day? Describe it. Is there something you still need to do as a result of this discovery? Ask the Lord...write it down...and then do it.

6) Aside from your personal "morning sickness" symptoms, what did you begin to experience on behalf of your spiritual child? Have you been able to carry them under the anointing and still express unconditional love to him or her? Make a list of your child's early symptoms and apply the Blood of Jesus to them in prayer—then let healing flow.

7) Remember each thing God has required you to walk through for your spiritual child. In everything, do you still see His hand? Write three reasons why you still have hope to carry this "baby" full term.

To the Prophet-in-the-Making

Have you fully accepted your spiritual parent into your heart and life? How has God confirmed this relationship to you? Have you continued to expose every area, no matter what, so that you can be healed?

Read Hebrews 4:1–16

Breakdown: Battle of the Mind

But there is another law at work within me that is at war with my mind.
This law wins the fight and makes me a slave
to the sin that is still within me.
—*Romans 7:23 NLT*

The Second Trimester Begins

At a certain stage of Juanita's spiritual development, I began to see evidence of mental distress and nervous breakdown. I watched her as she experienced schizophrenic tendencies and other serious personality problems. She dealt with bouts of anger and depression, as well as eating binges (especially cravings for sweets, and hot and spicy foods). Juanita was obviously angry and hurt...yet, God was still with her.

> **Juanita was obviously angry and hurt...yet, God was still with her.**

When demonic spirits would attack her, trying to abort her "birth," my husband and I would pray and cover her. Demons would literally leap down from the ceiling—tormenting her—trying to kill the prophetess. This became a constant ritual, almost a nightly battle, but we refused to let Satan have her. We felt like rookies, but we couldn't let the enemy take her out. (We'd been in ministry for a number of years, but this was the first time we'd ever gone through anything like this.)

Adding to the challenge, not only was I inexperienced in how to maintain my first "spiritual baby," I didn't know how to take care of myself, either. Clearly, I needed help for the journey. As time passed, I became more and more grateful to God for blessing me with a wise, sober-minded husband. He was always there, keeping me grounded and stable enough to carry this "baby" full term. I wouldn't have been able to do it alone...and together, we still knew that we couldn't do it without God's help.

Many times, my husband and I made mistakes, because we didn't know how to help Juanita. Yet, one element remained constant...our love for her. The mistakes we made were from our *heads* and not our *hearts.* Our motivation was always love—never vindictiveness or cruel intent.

Amidst all of this, people who didn't understand my calling to help Juanita began to come against me. I faced considerable ridicule, criticism, and persecution because of our relationship. It seemed everyone had an opinion about her place in my life, home, and spiritual womb. They falsely accused me of vile things...which bruised me deeply. Yet God the Father knew the truth. I was her spiritual mother. I was preparing Juanita for her ultimate ministry unto God. Even today, I still see her as my daughter—my "spiritual firstborn" into worldwide ministry.

The accusations also wounded Juanita. People verbally mistreated and "labeled" her in perverse ways. Yet, my family and I knew that Juanita was wholly a woman with a broken heart. She could never be any of the vile things that others labeled her as being.

Unfortunately, when Juanita sought physical solace, it was in the arms of men. She later wrote about her struggle with sex and quest for acceptance in her book, *No More Sheets.* I don't think I even have to say that God has used this book to set thousands of believers free from sexual bondage.

Step by step, the enemy assaulted Juanita's mind, never letting up or relinquishing his attacks—even for a moment. Once...very early in the morning...I found her sitting in the middle of my living room. It was the dead of winter. The house was cold because we always set the heating unit to shut off at 11:00 p.m. Juanita had wrapped herself in a blanket and was engaged in yet another eating binge. That morning, she was craving "Fireball" candies and popcorn saturated with hot sauce.

> **The enemy assaulted Juanita's mind, never letting up or relinquishing his attacks—even for a moment.**

Everyone was still asleep, and up until that moment, *so was I.* But like an alarm system in my spirit, the Holy Ghost awakened me, alerting me that something evil and demonic was in the house. Then I heard the television...so I got out of bed, knowing this was highly unusual.

When I entered the living room, Juanita was in a trancelike state, rocking violently back and forth. Like radar, the Holy Ghost opened her thoughts to me. I heard every vile, evil word as it flowed through her mind. And I knew those thoughts were not her own. Satan was telling her lies. The Holy Spirit exposed him! I quickly disrupted this state of mind by telling her about all the lies I heard the enemy speaking into her mind. This angered her immensely.

"I hate you!" she screamed. "I can't even *think* in this house!"

My husband and I immediately decided to begin deliverance sessions with Juanita. We had purchased a book entitled, *Pigs in the Parlor* by Frank and Ida Mae Hammond, which was more or less a manual on deliverance. It quickly became a map, guide, and necessary reference for us as we continued working with Juanita.

We learned from the book that we were dealing with more than one personality.

The book gave invaluable instruction on how to minister to her needs. It also emphasized that we shouldn't get involved in her storm (which truly was a whirlwind). That was my greatest area of struggle throughout Juanita's gestational period, because I hadn't yet mastered the ability to "*not*" become intertwined with her raging storms.

I didn't understand the difference between distancing myself from the tumult and staying close to Juanita. So I withdrew further away from her, with the intent of staying *outside* of what was going on *inside* of her.

Juanita experienced a sense of abandonment; she felt I had alienated and rejected her. Innocently, I thought distancing myself was necessary, without considering how it might harm her. I had good intentions and sincerely thought I was doing the right thing. In the end result, I realized to my regret that I had wrongly administered my good intentions toward Juanita.

Even still, in His infinite grace and wisdom, God remained faithful to us through this entire ordeal (which was indeed a learning experience for us all). He covered our mistakes with His mercy and restored us as only He could do.

> **God loved Juanita. He knew that she'd fulfill His divine purpose—no matter what!**

God loved Juanita—His daughter of destiny. Ultimately, He knew that she'd fulfill His divine purpose—no matter what! "Daddy" God protected her in areas where we had been foolish and during times we had left her uncovered.

In the midst of her deliverance, she continued to suffer from serious demonic attacks. At times, she'd get "lost" in her own mind. Then she'd start running around with men and eating heavily, which caused her to gain excessive weight and resulted in even lower self-esteem. Juanita hated herself and began to express that hatred outwardly. *The "baby" was screaming and crying out for help.*

The woman on the "outside" began to hate the prophetess on the "inside." She began to despise the call of God on her life and reasoned that the cost was too great to bear; so one day she declared, "It ain't worth it. I'm going to do my own thing. If I have to be a prophet my whole life, I'm going to go out and enjoy the world for a while." And that's what she did. But I have to say, even though she stepped out of the will of God, she never stopped coming to church. In her heart of hearts, Juanita knew she could never stray too far. The body of Christ was her lifeline.

Yes, the "baby" in my womb was attempting to abort her purpose in God. And it wasn't long before she ended up paying a heavy price for her decision. Juanita talked about this season of her life in *No More Sheets,* describing the terrible toll of this brief departure from God.

As she plunged deeper into sin, I saw her mind plunge deeper into oblivion. It literally sunk into its own reality. And though she could still function (somewhat) around the deception of her mind...Juanita could appear to be someone that she wasn't. Therein lies the danger! Juanita could manipulate her own existence and become a leader for "good" or "evil." She had the God-given ability to influence people, regardless of her state of mind. She could convince them to perform as instructed.

Other times, Juanita would flow in her "giftings" and help a lot of people. We saw that she was still able to touch the lives of others in a profound way. However, when the battle in her mind resurfaced, she became vulnerable enough to hurt others. Yes, "gifts" were definitely evident in her life, regardless of her own personal struggles. God used Juanita, whether she was right or wrong.

> **My husband told her that without character, integrity, and total dependence upon God, she couldn't properly maintain these gifts**

My husband made many attempts to counsel with Juanita about how important it is to be true to God, especially in the operation of her gifts. He told her that without character, integrity, and total dependence upon God, she couldn't properly maintain these gifts. It would end in disaster, both for her, and in the lives of those with whom she expressed her anointing. Over and over, my husband reiterated to her the spiritual reality of this truth.

Here's a good example of the character building process. One night, Juanita was driving around in her little yellow Volkswagen when she decided to stop at Red Shingles (a well-known bar in town) to "talk" to a "friend." Mind you, it was Saturday night. Before service the next morning, her spiritual dad already knew about where she'd been the night before—she'd been spotted.

Juanita had no idea anybody knew, so she came to church prepared to direct the choir, just like any other Sunday. However, before she could enter the sanctuary, Pastor requested her presence in his office. She was already in her robe and ready to go into the service. Later, she told us the thought, *What have I done now?* darted through her mind. When she entered my husband's office, her stomach dropped to her feet—*she already knew*. Without the need for explanation, Pastor told her to remove her robe and take a seat on the front row with the "church mothers." She was to sit there every service until he released her. *The mothers had always saved a seat for Juanita, because they knew sooner or later, she'd be joining them.*

These "church mothers" (of New Hope Tabernacle C.O.G.I.C.) were Juanita's prayer mentors. They were older women, full of wisdom, who loved her unreservedly. They taught her how to pray consistently and with perseverance. Each woman had a different, unique personality and qualities to offer in the process of her birthing. Each gave her a wonderful gift of incredible eternal value.

My mother, Margaret Hill, was the lead "prayer warrior" and midwife. She was the "fire" of the team—a pacesetter, trailblazer, and "devil driver." Juanita received her as a spiritual grandmother, and she loved Juanita as one of her own grandchildren...after all, she was our spiritual daughter. Mother respected the greatness she observed in "Sister Juanita." And she recognized it outwardly (like all the church mothers did).

Mother Katherlean Lott was the glue that held the team together. She was a woman of peace and calmness—a woman of God whose quiet confidence was her strength. Juanita saw Christ reflected in Mother Lott's life. Even until she went to be with the Lord (at age ninety-three), that same reflection emanated from within her.

Mother Florence Milan was the one who walked in great faith. She constantly encouraged Juanita to live by faith. She taught her

> **Pastor told her to remove her robe and take a seat on the front row with the "church mothers."**

> **As prayer mentors, all of the church mothers had a specific role in birthing Juanita.**

how to stand on the Word of God, believe Him for the impossible, and never move from that position...*no matter what.*

And then there was Mother Elizabeth Howell, who taught Juanita how to be poised, loving, and strong in her faith. She constantly reiterated the importance of standing firm on the Word of God, remaining "...stedfast, unmoveable, always abounding in the work of the Lord..." (1 Corinthians 15:58).

As prayer mentors, all of the church mothers had a specific role in birthing Juanita. Beyond this, they greatly influenced her future ministry by demonstrating to her that *nothing would be impossible to those who seek the face of the Lord.*

Throughout this process, I can sincerely say that Juanita kept the right attitude and remained obedient and faithful...even when she didn't want to. Whether she realized it or not, she was learning how to endure the chastening of the Lord (see Hebrews 12:5–6). Today, everyone can see the results of her obedience. God awesomely uses her. When I witness the magnitude of her ministry, I lift up praises to Him.

Yes, many times we were imperfect in how we handled our spiritual daughter during this time, but in everything, Juanita understood that our love and motives toward her were perfect... because they were rooted in God.

Reflection and Study

1) Have you seen signs of distress and breakdown in your spiritual son or daughter? What are they?

2) What is your understanding of deliverance ministry? Would you be willing to seek God and become more knowledgeable in this area, for the sake of your pregnancy? What has God revealed to you in intercession about these strongholds?

3) How have you handled any persecutions and false accusations concerning you and your spiritual child? Do you get embarrassed? Angry? In spite of this, can you still see the true state of your child's heart? Have your words, attitudes, and actions demonstrated God's love…no matter what? If not, how can you correct them?

4) What are your "baby's" specific struggles? With Juanita, men were a major struggle. How do you think you can deal with these situations without distancing yourself from your child?

5) What character building processes have you administered to your protégé? Did you stick by them? Why or why not? Have you seen a difference in your child's life?

6) Who else in your church family is actively part of the birthing process? Write down their names and what they contribute to his or her spiritual development. Are any areas uncovered?

7) In fighting the spiritual abortion process within your son or daughter, have you ever been tempted to give up? Have you kept yourself under divine counsel? Do you still see God's hand in this process, and believe His purpose will ultimately be fulfilled? Why or why not?

To the Prophet-in-the-Making

Are you struggling against destructive thoughts and accusations? In spite of this, are you willing to do what your spiritual parents require of you, no matter how difficult it may seem to be?

Read Hebrews 12:1–13

Survival of the Fittest

I shall not die but live, and shall declare the works *and* recount the illustrious acts of the Lord.
—*Psalm 118:17* AMPL

Juanita fought with God and herself. The constant battles drove her into a low place—to the point of poverty. According to Proverbs 13:15, "...the way of transgressors *is* hard." This became a living testimonial of Juanita's lifestyle. She moved out of our home and ended up living in "low-income" housing, better known as "the projects." She had meager furnishings...a kitchen table and a couple of chairs. Yet, this was all part of the process of being chosen "in the furnace of affliction" according to Isaiah 48:10. With every step, Juanita was being formed in the "womb."

Although she had moved out, Juanita was still very much a part of me. I made sure she still lived in the haven of my spiritual "womb" by continuing to cover her spiritually and physically. Sometimes the thought disturbed me: *My "baby" owns nothing!* In so many ways, Juanita was "naked" in her existence. So we fed, clothed, and took care of her, like parents tending to an infant. She stayed with us many nights, and our door was always open. We never denied Juanita entrance when it was in our power to help her.

> **Although she had moved out, Juanita was still very much a part of me.**

However, there were times when God wouldn't allow us to come to her aid. And this is difficult to admit. Sometimes, as parents, we were unable to protect her. But there were also times when God didn't want her to be "overly" protected. He wanted us to release her into His hands. We often struggled in this area. We were still learning what it meant to become spiritual parents.

The burden became especially hard when Juanita attempted suicide. *Our daughter wanted to die!* And it was extremely difficult to convince her otherwise. The enemy had her believing that death was better than life. Satan was on a mission to destroy her—to wipe her off the face of the earth before she could impact more lives for the kingdom.

> **The enemy had her believing that death was better than life. Satan was on a mission to destroy her.**

He wanted to *snuff her out...he wanted Juanita to be dead and gone before she could fulfill her destiny in God!*

Yet, God, the eternal and loving Father, proclaimed: "NOT SO!"

With every suicide attempt, God intervened in some miraculous way. He intended for Juanita Bynum to remain on the earth for His divine purpose. She was called to a specific time and for a particular people...*the nations*. Therefore, no devil in hell could thwart God's plan for her life! He had called her to birth out a holy people, who would seek after Him and His holiness...people who would desire to live "Behind the Veil."

God wouldn't let her go!

Even so, that didn't stop Juanita from trying to drown herself in the river a block away from her house, or later attempting to overdose on prescription blood pressure medication. During the attempted overdose, God allowed my family (especially my husband), to save her from an untimely demise.

It sobers me to this day when I think of it. The blood pressure pills belonged to my husband. And one day, Juanita came into the house specifically looking for them. She said, "Hello" as she reached our bedroom door, and then went into the bathroom. Strangely, she left the house without saying goodbye; we were clueless about what had transpired in the bathroom. However, our oldest daughter Cherise had a sinking suspicion that something was desperately wrong.

"I think you'd better check the medicine cabinet. I think Juanita did something," she warned.

It didn't go unheeded. Immediately, I checked the bathroom and noticed that a bottle of Dad's blood pressure pills had been tampered with. Nearly all of the pills were gone! *Juanita had taken them!*

I ran and told my husband...he jumped out of bed, threw on his clothes, and scrambled to the car. He knew better than anyone that he had to find Juanita before it was too late. He figured that she probably

> **"I think you'd better check the medicine cabinet. I think Juanita did something," she warned.**

hadn't gone very far...*and he was right.* When he spotted her, she was staggering down the street just a few blocks from our house.

Juanita was getting dangerously close to one of the busiest thoroughfares in Port Huron—Electric Avenue. My husband pulled up behind her, slammed on the brakes, and jumped out of the car. God's timing was perfect. As he grabbed her waist and scooped her up to safety, she was about to step in the path of a speeding semi-truck! Only her shoes were left in the middle of the street...seconds later, the semi whizzed by and flattened them into the pavement.

William took Juanita straight to the Emergency Room to get her stomach pumped. After they'd given her some medication to counteract the effects of the blood pressure pills, they put her in the Psychiatric Ward for a few days of observation. Many saints were praying along with our family, interceding specifically for our spiritual daughter's destiny. The church mothers (and all of the intercessors) covered Juanita with prayer. *A corporate cry of travail went up for her!*

After Juanita recovered, I gave her a pair of my diamond earrings as a memento of our deep love for her. We went to great lengths to help Juanita become all that God wanted her to be. Somehow, I still knew beyond the shadow of a doubt that God had brought her into our lives.

There were many other occasions when our resolve to birth out this prophet-in-the-making was tested. We constantly had to remind ourselves that our connection with her was God's will. That being said, a time arrived when we needed some space apart. We decided to send her to Chicago for a few days.

The trip turned out to be more than her friends, Marty and Debbie (who were driving her), had bargained for. Normally, the trip should have taken four-and-a-half to five hours. But as it turned out, it took almost *twelve*. Juanita kept trying to jump out of the car, so they constantly had to pull over to keep her from being killed on the highway. Every time they stopped the car, she'd jump out and run down the road. Marty or Debbie would then chase her down and force her back into the car. This ritual continued all the way to Chicago.

Juanita's friends hoped that she'd be able to stay with her parents for a while. However, this wasn't God's plan and she soon returned to Port Huron. The battle within intensified. One particular time (during the summer), I remember it being quite warm outside, and Juanita was spotted walking around aimlessly in a winter coat. Thankfully, an older gentleman, Brother Willie—who knew her and the church she attended—stopped to see if she was okay. Upon closer inspection, he noticed that she looked lost, dazed, and confused...*she was unable to remember who or where she was.*

Beside the fact that she was wearing a winter coat on a hot day, Juanita's hair was a mess, which was totally uncharacteristic of her. She was virtually in a trancelike state. Thanks be to God, though, for sending someone who was willing to help, not harm, our spiritual daughter. Somehow, Brother Willie convinced Juanita to get into his car and then he drove her to our house. Immediately, we began to cast out the spirit of insanity and minister deliverance to her troubled soul.

> **She still had to let go of a lot of hurt and pain from her past, but she was neither willing nor ready to release it.**

Although Juanita overcame that *battle*, the *war* was far from over. She still had to let go of a lot of hurt and pain from her past, but she was neither *willing* nor *ready* to release it. She continued trying to find someone—*anyone*—to alleviate the nagging pain in her "damaged" heart. It was obvious there were still areas she hadn't surrendered to God. Yet, amazingly, she had come to the point that she was able to be honest with me...her spiritual mother...once again.

Juanita began to share with me about times when she'd slept with men. And when she didn't tell me about it, God would reveal it to me. Whenever God exposed her weak areas, I'd go to her and she'd openly and honestly confess. This openness didn't come without its fair share of battles. Maintaining a grown woman in the "womb" was hard work. Often, I was very hard on her...not mincing words or cutting corners...I felt I had to be rigid.

I remembered my own mentoring as a young woman, under the tutelage of my pastor's wife, Mother Lena Mason Lucas. She had been unbending and rigid with me (as well as my mother) as she endeavored to shape me into the woman God destined for me to become. I found myself being as she had "been," a representative of her spiritual guidance. As a young woman, I was totally impressed by Mother Lucas as she poured from her life into me...I was so hungry to be fed by and learn from her. So in my life, both my "natural" and "spiritual" mothers left their legacy inside of me.

> **I had to be unbending at times, even though it caused friction between Juanita and me.**

Now I had my own spiritual daughter to mentor and raise up to maturity. I had a life to shape. Therefore, I had to be unbending at times, even though it caused friction between Juanita and me. Ultimately, this constant friction sealed our connection. Finally, Juanita and I were attached by a "spiritual umbilical cord." (Much like an umbilical cord in the natural realm, our "spiritual cord" supplied nourishment to Juanita's spirit and began the process of eliminating all of the spiritual wastes and poisons that had been introduced into her system.)

Carrying this prophet in the womb of the Spirit transformed both Juanita and me into different people. I was learning how to be a spiritual mother—a true mother in Zion that would eventually understand how to mentor and carry many more "babies" to full term.

(I can honestly say *I am that mother* now, as a result of my experience with Juanita. The first child always teaches a mother how to take on her maternal spirit and accept everything it brings without fear or anxiety.)

God was also teaching Juanita how to become a true spiritual daughter. This learning process was tiring and intense. Many times, I can remember her questioning all of the stress she had to endure during her gestational period. She hadn't yet become fully aware of why the process we were enduring was necessary (though she came to this understanding later).

Also, Juanita and I couldn't be considered "friends" in the natural sense, because her future hinged on both of us being true to our roles as purposed by God. Her future literally hung in the balance. It depended upon her ability to obey me as her *mother* in the Spirit, not to relate to me as a casual acquaintance.

Juanita most definitely "learned obedience" through the things she suffered (see Hebrews 5:8). She learned submission by deciding to respond in a godly way to spiritual authority—choosing not to forfeit her future through rebellion. Obedience is why she's living and walking in her inheritance right now.

Day by day, Juanita learned how to become the "daughter" God desired!

Day by day, Juanita learned how to become the "daughter" God desired! He brought her into "sonship" through total obedience and submission to His will. And she gradually reached the state where (being mentored), she recognized that even in adulthood, she was still a child in training.

Yes, within the context of our relationship, I realized that as the bodies of both mother and child change shape during pregnancy, both Juanita and I were being molded into vessels of honor.

> But in a great house there are not only vessels of gold and of silver, but also of wood and of earth; and some to honour, and some to dishonour. If a man therefore purge himself from these, he shall be a vessel unto honour, sanctified, and meet for the master's use, *and* prepared unto every good work.
> —*2 Timothy 2:20–21*

Reflection and Study

1) Has God ever required you to withhold help from your spiritual son or daughter? Were you obedient? How did you cope with it?

2) Has your spiritual child ever attempted to take his or her own life? If so, how did God intervene in that situation? How did God get the victory?

3) Can you see a pattern of how the enemy has been trying to stop the spiritual birthing process in your prophet-in-the-making? Write it down, and then let God lead you into intercession.

4) Have you been able to take a time of rest to renew your mind and spirit? If not, how could you make this happen? Write a tentative plan.

5) How are you adjusting to your responsibilities as a spiritual parent? What areas need to be strengthened?

6) In what ways do you see your "spiritual baby" developing into a true spiritual son or daughter? Write down a few of the areas where you've seen the most progress. Make notes about his or her weak areas for intercession, to receive further direction from God.

7) During this gestation process, have you and your child been able to maintain open communication? How do you respond when he or she confides in you, sharing things you'd be more comfortable not knowing?

To the Prophet-in-the-Making

Have you been running from God, trying to escape your destiny? Stop running from the process and let God minister to your spirit. Let Him shape you into a vessel of honor.

Read Jonah 1–4
and Proverbs 13:15–18

The Death Walk

I assure you, most solemnly I tell you, Unless a grain of wheat
falls into the earth and dies, it remains [just one grain; it never becomes more
but lives] by itself alone. But if it dies, it produces many others
and yields a rich harvest.
—*John 12:24* AMPL

Everyone has a final breaking point. You never know which situation could be the catalyst that brings it to the surface, but it's waiting there nonetheless. Even after attempting suicide, when it seemed it couldn't get any worse, an even darker season came for Juanita. It was the day she faced herself, once and for all. Like Jacob, she was now wrestling for her future destiny in the kingdom.

> **Juanita had arrived at Bethel—her place of testing, trial, and tribulation.**

Juanita had arrived at Bethel—her place of testing, trial, and tribulation (see Genesis 35). Now, she'd either surrender to the call or lose everything.

In many ways, this spiritual pregnancy was now exhibiting the same danger signs as when a natural fetus develops inside of its mother's fallopian tube. You see, Satan was always trying to destroy Juanita in the womb. Time after time, he tried to make me miscarry—because he knew she was going to wreak havoc in his kingdom when she was finally birthed out. At times, it seemed like Juanita was trapped in a vice grip with no way to turn, except to escape prematurely from the place she was being formed.

Total Breakdown

One of Satan's attacks came by way of a nervous breakdown. Oh, yes, he was desperately trying to destroy Juanita, but God turned it around for her good. He allowed her to "break down" into a state of absolute humility, and then drove her to her knees in total submission unto Him.

I understood the place Juanita was in, because I had suffered a stress breakdown a few years earlier. And actually, God used her during that time to encourage and strengthen me, even in the midst of her own struggle: the signs of a true prophet. Juanita would come and spend time with me daily...her presence was a ministry to me. She'd cook my favorite meals, style my hair, and speak words of life—even staying at my bedside for days rebuking the spirit of death. During this time, Juanita would speak prophetically to me without even realizing it. She demonstrated her love by her actions. Indeed, we had both paid a high price, but this death process wrought deeper purification in our souls.

The prophet's life was on the line, and so was the ministry lying dormant inside of her. Yet, again, God watched over her and protected the treasure He'd invested in this "daughter of destiny." Under the layers of grief, God had planted His purpose deep inside of Juanita...but it wasn't time for it to come forth. He wanted to bring increase in every area of Juanita's life, but first, she had to go through the "planting" process. In other words, she was still developing the necessary elements needed to survive the life she was destined to embrace.

> **The prophet's life was on the line, and so was the ministry lying dormant inside of her.**

During this planting process, the seed that had once represented her life had to be cast into the earth to die. So during this stage of prenatal development, certain parts of her "old nature" had to be put to death—*and then be buried for good.* Old patterns of iniquity that caused her to fall into sexual sin had to be purged completely, or she would continue in this destructive cycle of the flesh. And this wouldn't be easy.

The Third Trimester

In many ways, this experience was not unlike the "valley of the shadow of death" that David described in Psalm 23. Juanita was in a place where she felt alone, afraid, and abandoned. This is the death walk, the place where "unforeseen complications" can arise late in the gestational process. It is a solitary experience. Like Lazarus, you

> **Juanita was in a place where she felt alone, afraid, and abandoned.**

reek of the stench of death in this valley, but when Jesus calls you forth, death has to release its "grip" (see John 11:41–44).

It seemed this would be her walk for an eternity. As she "came forth," the dead, rotten parts of her existence were being washed away...one by one. All that would ultimately remain would be the parts that were fit for the Master's use.

As illustrated above in John 12:24, God wants all of His children to become like the "grain of wheat." Therefore, we must die in order to produce spiritual fruit. He didn't design us to live our existence as a "single seed," without producing anything for His glory. So when a seed is planted, the protective outer shell must be *broken* in order to release the *harvest that's developing inside.* Did you know that a single seed planted in nutrient-rich soil could literally produce a plentiful harvest of fruit? Spiritually, it's the same process—death produces life!

Jesus continued in John 12:25, "Anyone who loves his life loses it, but anyone who hates his life in this world will keep it to life eternal. [Whoever has no love for, no concern for, no regard for his life here on earth, but despises it, preserves his life forever and ever.]" AMPL. This is why, as believers, we must never be afraid to give our lives away, even to the point of death. We must not resist death, for it is through "death to self" that we are able to produce many "new lives." For Juanita, it has become evident that when she died to her own desires, it literally birthed a plethora of new lives for the kingdom of God. Now, she understands completely why her death walk was necessary.

> **This was a pivotal time in her walk. She literally had to rely on others to see God's destiny for her life.**

During the breakdown, however, she couldn't see her purpose or destiny...she only saw death. Yet, she remained faithful and obedient to her spiritual parents, and most of all to God. I witnessed how He gave her the grace and strength to "...endure hardness, as a good soldier of Jesus Christ," *despite the things she still couldn't see.* (See 2 Timothy 2:3.) This was a pivotal time in her walk. She literally had to rely on others to see God's destiny for her life. She had to be constantly encouraged to stay the course and remain in the race toward fulfilling the purposes of God.

Anorexia Nervosa

The fight took its toll on her physically as Juanita faced more attacks from the prince of darkness. Satan decided to step up his strategic assault against her mind and body by plotting to starve her to death with Anorexia. Just before this attack, however, she was having an affair (of sorts) with a man who lived out of state...against our desires and instructions. This time, it took longer for Juanita to respond; she *"delayed"* her obedience. And, yes, by doing this she left herself wide open for an attack. By the time Juanita submitted to our direction, the *spirit of anorexia* had already pounced upon her—and it was determined to overtake and steal her life away. (Ironically, the enemy had attempted to do the same thing to me during a weak point in my life.)

Juanita had gotten involved with this man as a result of her battle with the spirit of rejection, which had already proven to be a stronghold in her life. You see, Juanita was angry. In many ways, *anger* had invited *rejection* to come in. The spirit of rejection had stepped up its quest to completely destroy Juanita by any means necessary.

It seemed she just didn't care anymore. I didn't realize then she was emotionally worn out from ministering to me only a few weeks earlier, so she was susceptible to satanic attack. Juanita was vulnerable, spiritually and otherwise. She felt alone and helpless without my strength...so she fell prey to the weakness of her flesh and, once again, sought the solace of security according to her old pattern of iniquity. She landed in the arms of yet another man. One night, my husband and I caught her sitting in the car outside of her apartment with this same man—*another attempt at rebellion.*

She soon fell prey to the "demon of anorexia" as the warfare raged against her. I believe this spirit attacked her because she was inside of my spiritual womb—so she was a part of me. When I was battling with this same spirit during my breakdown, Juanita had helped me to overcome; yet, she fell victim to it because of disobedience and delayed repentance.

> **She soon fell prey to the "demon of Anorexia" as the warfare raged against her.**

Three weeks after I was healed and delivered, Juanita fell prey to the same attack. This vile spirit became "familiar" to both of us, because we were connected. So as I was growing stronger and more able to handle the enemy, Juanita was becoming weaker. This spirit was looking for another home, and because Juanita's defenses were down (due to rebellion), she became accessible.

We knew that if Juanita didn't fight against this diabolical attack of the enemy, her body would surely die. (During times of intense spiritual and mental warfare, it's vital to stay strong physically.) It takes *physical* and *spiritual* strength to fight these battles. So if Satan can get you chemically imbalanced from a lack of nourishment, it increases the effects of mental anguish and leaves you an "open target" for his devices.

> **As far as the enemy was concerned, we weren't going to get our daughter back. But, thank God, Satan can never have the last word!**

My husband and I went to Juanita while she was in the midst of her anguish…to set her free…cast that demon out of her body, and her life, for good. During this confrontation, the spirit declared that he was going to kill her. He proclaimed ownership over her. As far as the enemy was concerned, we weren't going to get our daughter back. But, thank God, Satan can never have the last word! God's Word and His will have preeminence.

Finally, Juanita gave up that ungodly affair—*without resistance*—and the enemy had no choice but to relinquish his hold on her. She emerged from this having learned a valuable lesson...one we'd all do well to remember: "...to obey *is* better than sacrifice..." (see 1 Samuel 15:22). The key is, *obey God immediately,* because *delayed obedience* can cost your life.

Juanita had other suicide episodes, but through it all, God kept His eye on her. He protected Juanita (even from herself) for the sake of the generation she would impact for His glory. Satan's repeated assaults during those nine years proved the path that lay before her was of great significance...not only to the kingdom of Light, but also to the kingdom of darkness.

> **During the time of her breaking, God was in the process of "making me"...**

Inside of my spiritual womb, the baby was kicking "the hell out of me." *I mean that literally.* Juanita wanted to be free! God had ordained total and complete freedom for her. She desperately needed it, and she had to obtain that freedom *within herself.* I, too, wanted freedom. And interestingly, during the time of her breaking, God was in the process of "making me" as well.

At this point, familiarity became our enemy. My husband and I had become so close to Juanita and so familiar with her struggles that we began to take some of the things she was experiencing for granted. We didn't realize the level of warfare we were in; it was as if the outer, protective shell of our covering over Juanita was splitting. We didn't understand the serious implications of her breakdown until it was nearly too late. We almost didn't take the pain she was in seriously. Instead, we considered our baby's "kicks" to be just a normal part of the growth process.

For example, she'd often change her hairstyle from one extreme to another...sometimes on a weekly basis. But instead of being normal, it was actually something quite different. Often, it meant something drastic was about to occur. She would either be in the process of a rebellious act, or of going away in her mind. Then she'd alienate herself from us altogether. And before we knew it, Juanita would be running around with unsavory people that drew her even deeper into this destructive cycle. No, these "kicks" weren't normal development for a daughter of destiny.

It seemed Juanita was unable to receive her total deliverance through us as her spiritual parents. *She resented us.* Juanita didn't believe we were genuinely concerned about her well-being. Sometimes, we'd procrastinate and miss opportunities to show her how much we really cared. We were so close to her that we couldn't always see the depths of her struggle. Therefore, as far as she was concerned, our movements were too slow.

I saw a little girl in a woman's body trying to get out...wanting to make it on her own...no longer wanting to be told what to do. This little girl was trapped inside of my spiritual fallopian tube; she felt smothered, suppressed, fearful, and angry. Juanita wanted to be released; she wanted to escape! Yet she had to first break free of the torment (i.e., the evidence of Satan's bondage in her life). Her spirit could not, and would not, be contained. Though her ability to lead was obvious, my husband would have to remove her from ministry whenever iniquity rose up. God was still at work in her, taking diligent care of His daughter, and protecting her spirit. Yes, He was literally changing, rearranging, and transforming her into a new, "freer" woman.

The process of Juanita's breakdown replayed itself over and over. She constantly lived on the edge of turmoil, ready to break at any moment. Because of her delicate emotional state, we weren't certain how she might respond when confronted or corrected. Finally, however, Juanita came to the end of herself. And when her deliverance emerged, she was instantly freed from Anorexia. (This took place when God led Juanita to attend a church service in Detroit

> **When her deliverance emerged, she was instantly freed from Anorexia.**

where a woman full of the Spirit of God discerned her struggle and cast the devil out of her.) The "torment" was over!

Light finally started to shine through the darkness in my "womb" and the kicking stopped. Yet, our "baby" still wanted to leave. She wanted to fully emerge from the place of formation. Still, God wouldn't let her veer off too far before He settled her right back into position in the "womb." Now that she was "free," Juanita had to learn how to be still, get to know the Lord again, and embrace His total plan for her life.

Only God could determine how much time it would take to complete this difficult process. He knew Juanita intrinsically on a much deeper level. (By the way, this is why she's adopted the song, "Be Still and Know that I am God." No one else can sing it with as much definition as she can, because she "walked it out" during the final stages of her gestational period.) When Juanita's birthing was complete, being still and waiting quietly upon God would become the "earmark" of her ministry. This is how she finally learned to hear His voice clearly...how she made it through the "furnace of affliction" to become a true prophet to the nations.

Reflection and Study

1) Has your spiritual son or daughter arrived at Bethel? What is his or her final breaking point?

2) At the same time, have you been experiencing "third trimester" discomforts? What do you believe God wants you to do to "make room" for the baby that's struggling to be released? List a few, practical steps you may need to take.

3) Which "seeds" have to die inside of this prophet-in-the-making for new life to be released? What patterns of behavior must die? Write them down, and then make intercession before the Lord.

4) In what ways have you felt you've been unable to cover this child of destiny? Is it just part of this stage of gestation, or do you need to examine yourself and adjust in some areas?

5) Write about your single most intense spiritual battle up to this point. Can you see the intervention and deliverance of God coming forth? How?

6) Which "strongmen" are coming down in the developing prophet's life? In yours? Put them under the Blood for good, and then praise God for deliverance.

7) Have both you and your spiritual child embraced the process of becoming still before God? If not, what's standing in the way?

To the Prophet-in-the-Making

What "seeds" need to die in your life so that your
spirit can be released into divine destiny?
Whatever it is, let it go.

*Study Genesis 35:1–15
and John 12:20–36*

Key to Deliverance...Submission

Submit yourselves therefore to God. Resist the devil,
and he will flee from you.
James 4:7

Juanita was truly learning the value of submission. Through every stage of development, her understanding deepened. We could see that the relevance and necessity of submitting to my husband and me as her "spiritual authorities" was becoming clearer in her spirit. Coupled with this, Juanita had already learned the value of persevering in

> **Through every stage of development, her understanding deepened.**

prayer from our "church mothers." So when she was faced with the choice to either obey or disobey, she started choosing obedience. She already knew the consequences of disobedience were far too high a price to pay. This had been deeply rooted within her. Our "baby" began to grow and mature in the ways of God...she was becoming a model of true worship.

> ...let us lay aside every weight, and the sin which doth so easily beset *us*, and let us run with patience the race that is set before us, Looking unto Jesus the author and finisher of *our* faith; who for the joy that was set before him endured the cross...
> *Hebrews 12:1 2*

Not unlike Jesus, Juanita had learned obedience through the things she suffered. She discovered (as we all do eventually), that in order to become a "joint-heir" with Christ, we must be willing to share in His sufferings. In her spirit, Juanita finally knew that if she endured afflictions, her reward would be great. Still, this was easier said than done. It's costly to live "behind the veil." You don't just get to that place; you have to go through the process of purification to *enter in.* During this new season (later in the third trimester), Juanita learned to run to the Master in prayer and worship to gain strength for the race He had set before her.

As her spiritual growth progressed, "afflictions" started to come in the form of persecution. Looking back, this was an undeniable part of her developmental process. She endured constant pressure as God opened her eyes to her true identity in the Spirit. Persecutions came from both the natural and spiritual realms. Yet according to 2 Timothy 3:12, "...all that will live godly in Christ Jesus shall suffer persecution." So it was clear. Persecution was part of her "making," and ultimately, it would be a test of her commitment to God's call upon her life.

> **As her spiritual growth progressed, "afflictions" started to come in the form of persecution.**

God knew that Juanita had to go *through the fire* in order to remain *in Him.* This was extremely difficult for her. Juanita had to "pray without ceasing" to maintain intimate worship and keep her sanity (see Ephesians 6:18). During this gestational phase, she had to *crucify her flesh* through prayer and fasting. We watched Juanita endure the afflictions that were shaping and forcing her to grow up in Christ.

Through it all, she began to rely on us more and more as her spiritual parents. She was finally trusting and depending on us as a true spiritual daughter. (The level of her attachment is normally considered rare, but was necessary for the development of the "international" ministry God had placed inside of her.)

Knowing this, I took my role seriously. Juanita was a dynamic force! Her blend of brilliance, genius, and intellect—combined powerfully with her prophetic anointing—constantly pushed me to another level in God. As her mentor, it was important for me to stay at least one step ahead (spiritually) in order to effectively minister to her needs. I had to have "been there" and "done that" already in order to fully understand our daughter. Juanita constantly challenged me spiritually; so really, we sharpened one another.

A Spiritual Lineage

I couldn't afford to go into premature labor, because this special "baby" had to complete the full gestation for the sake of her future. With the Holy Spirit's tutelage during this first spiritual pregnancy, I was ever learning how to take care of Juanita and myself. Ultimately, she wouldn't be an "only child." Therefore, I had to master the necessary skills to successfully birth other "sons and daughters in the Spirit." There would be more, though not quite like her. Many children would be pushed out into destiny through my "spiritual birth canal" after spending the required time in the "womb." Each would be uniquely essential to God's kingdom.

Instinctively, I knew that any child who would come through my "womb" would be part of our spiritual lineage. As a prophetess, I would produce prophets and prophetesses (or those with a prophetic edge). The spiritual reproduction process is the same as in the natural. Just like human beings can only reproduce human beings (and not plants or animals), prophets can only fully reproduce after their own kind.

God has anointed me to touch the lives of many people, but when it comes to the "birthing process," the DNA blueprint for prophetic continuance lies within my genetic make-up. Therefore, I learned that I could only bring forth, from the "womb" of the Spirit, reproduction that is a part of my own experience in God.

Lessons Learned

Juanita, my first spiritual child, taught me a lot about myself and what God wanted to develop inside of me. He wanted to broaden my borders and "stretch me out" within to bring forth "multiple births." During our experience with her, the capacity for ministry was deepened within both my husband and me. Ministering to Juanita opened up a whole new world for us. We began to understand ministry in a way that we'd never encountered before. It was new and challenging, and we were hungry for it. Seeing someone metamorphose right before our eyes, knowing that God had used us in a significant role to release the end result, was very exciting.

During the entire span of spiritual pregnancy, my husband and I were shepherds over a ministry and pastors of an active church. Yet, God saw fit to deepen our pastoral understanding in terms of our role as "spiritual parents" in team ministry. Through it all, He was preparing both of us to help take the body of Christ to new heights.

Juanita was our first opportunity to truly love on a deeper, more intimate level—just as parents love and mentor their natural child. On the other hand, Juanita was to "learn ministry" by being deeply ministered to on a "one-on-one basis." We knew her well, and she embraced the opportunity to know us as parents. In short, we all learned together.

As it turned out, Juanita would be the only child we'd walk with in this manner. It was God ordained. We know now that we can never be like that with anyone else. At times, we were *too* close—so we couldn't see the forest for the trees—and that's when it was difficult to be objective. Ultimately, God knew exactly what He was doing. We believe our relationship with Juanita was His design. Everything happened according to His plan.

With Juanita, God gave us invaluable insight into true deliverance ministry. At the grassroots level, this ministry later became a part of our lives. But we weren't looking to establish a deliverance ministry—Juanita was our spiritual child, and we wanted her free. It was as simple as that. Please understand: Deliverance

> **With Juanita, God gave us invaluable insight into true deliverance ministry.**

ministry should always be the result of a quest to see broken and hurting people set free…people God loves and desires to use for His glory. Therefore, William and I couldn't afford to sit back and watch such a beautifully anointed woman miss out on the opportunity to become all God intended.

Juanita needed to be set free from all oppression—spiritually, mentally, emotionally, and physically. Yet when we met her, she was suppressing the anointing and calling on her life because she was bound up by iniquity. When we submitted to God and walked through the birthing process with Juanita, it birthed our deliverance ministry. Now, we've fully embraced it. It's a large part of our ministry. And the same thing happened with Juanita. She also embraced deliverance as a vital part of her ministry. The breakthrough that came in Juanita's life prepared each of us for the "freedom ministry" God had in store.

Deliverance ministry had made such a dynamic impact on Juanita's development as a prophet that we realized *without it* there wouldn't have been an opportunity for her to grow. This made us realize that deliverance had to be fully implemented into every aspect of our church's ministry. And when God would bring other individuals to us who were in need of spiritual parenting, deliverance would need to be woven into every stage of mentoring.

While we *recognized* the need for freedom in Juanita's life, *she had to step out* and grasp it. In other words, Juanita had to take an active part in her own deliverance. This is why prayer and worship played a significant part in her obtaining spiritual freedom. When she began to hunger after the things of God more than the things of this world, step by step, God began to change her focus. It's vital to seek God's face in the quest for true freedom. While He does use other people, like my husband and me, God is ultimately the One who delivers and sets us free.

In terms of spiritual pregnancy, deliverance can be likened to the elimination of waste in the natural body. While in the womb, a baby generates waste during gestation and rids these byproducts through its mother's umbilical cord. Danger quickly arises when these wastes cannot be eliminated. If these poisons remain inside the womb, or aren't successfully expelled, it can contaminate the baby, and even risk death. When a baby is being birthed, it begins to eliminate waste on its own—therefore, the mother has to release this child from the womb at exactly the right time...or the child could be permanently disabled.

The same is true for spiritual pregnancy. It's natural for spiritual waste to develop as the "fetus" grows. Demonic strongholds and/or our carnal nature (that exist in the flesh) can represent waste. During gestation, the mother's system must eliminate them, or the spiritual child could end up being deformed or even die in the womb. Deliverance, whether during spiritual development or during the birthing process, is the channel through which God cleanses the protégé's environment—*inside and out.* Either way, spiritual parents play a major role in removing things that can hinder their child's growth.

> **Demonic strongholds and our carnal nature can represent "waste." Deliverance is the channel through which God cleanses.**

The process of deliverance, while not very pretty, is the one element that can ensure healthy growth and development in a pregnancy. A blockage can cause death if it's not removed from the system. Blockages (either in the child or the mother) not only retain waste, but can also prevent nourishment from reaching the child…so just because a child is in the "womb" doesn't mean it's completely safe from harm. The womb is a haven, a place of development; there's no guarantee that it will be a total sanctuary. Many things can go wrong, especially if something is physically wrong with the mother—that's why I had to constantly rely upon the Great Physician during my spiritual pregnancy. Sometimes, you don't know how healthy a child will be until after he or she has come through labor and delivery.

> **It took time for her to break free from all of the pain, hurt, sin, and oppression.**

Juanita experienced spiritual blockages during my pregnancy. It took time for her to break free from all of the pain, hurt, sin, and oppression. Therefore, my husband and I had to be firm and let her know that holding onto all that "waste" would cost her future. She had to *want* to pursue God with her whole heart to fully obtain her freedom. During gestation, Juanita had help in releasing all the waste and garbage through my umbilical cord (that's why I often experienced the pain when she did).

But when the time of birthing came, she had to start functioning on her own and let God cleanse her. That's why prayer and worship were an essential part of her spiritual process.

> Therefore, since these [great] promises are ours, beloved, let us cleanse ourselves from everything that contaminates *and* defiles body and spirit, and bring [our] consecration to completeness in the [reverential] fear of God.
> —*2 Corinthians 7:1* AMPL

It's Only a Matter of Time

For each prophet, the length of time it takes during gestation to complete spiritual cleansing varies. With each new "baby," we found the process of deliverance was different. Juanita's time of cleansing wasn't the same length as others, *but she needed the time we put into her.* We had to apply special procedures so that God could use Juanita to impact the nations. In other words, she needed a radical cleansing—every door had to be shut, every area in her heart and mind renewed, renovated, healed, and consecrated, before the Master could thrust her into her destiny.

Today, as we watch Juanita minister before multitudes, we realize why her process was so intrusive and extensive. *She had to be emptied out before she could be filled to overflowing.* Now, Juanita is being poured out as a "drink offering" unto God's people. She couldn't be walking in this calling had she not accepted the "cup" that was set before her more than twenty years ago.

At times, it seemed the downward cycles were unending, but God broke them one-by-one. And at other times, I thought I'd lost her; but God always delivered Juanita from satanic onslaughts that were threatening to destroy her. Finally, God captured her heart...and the "old Juanita" moved out of the way.

Reflection and Study

1) Has your spiritual son or daughter learned the value of submission? In what ways has he or she started to "quickly obey" your instructions?

2) How does your protégé deal with persecution? Do you see the peaceable "fruit" of the Holy Spirit working in him or her? In what "new ways" are you starting to see your child seek after God?

3) How does your "baby" challenge you spiritually? Do you find, in fact, that you're "sharpening" each other, much like Juanita and me?

4) Do you have a confirmed prophetic anointing upon your life? List a few areas God has proven you in the Spirit that will be imparted into the life and ministry of your spiritual son or daughter.

5) Looking back on your spiritual pregnancy, how has God developed not only your relationship with your child, but each of your ministries? Are others benefiting from the lessons you've learned? How is God expanding your vision for ministry?

6) Write a few lessons you've learned about true love throughout this spiritual birthing process.

7) How is your protégé taking an active role in his or her deliverance?

To the Prophet-in-the-Making

Have you experienced a renewed desire to seek
after God in prayer and worship? Has
submission deepened in your life?

Read James 4:1–10

The Accusers

And I heard a loud voice saying in heaven...for the accuser
of our brethren is cast down, which accused them
before our God day and night.
—*Revelation 12:10*

The onslaught of attacks against Juanita didn't always come in the form of "unseen" encounters with the enemy. Some of the attempted "womb assassinations" came in a far deadlier form—*from other people.*

Thinking back to the mid-eighties, New Hope Tabernacle was experiencing awesome manifestations and visitations from God. About that same time, four self-proclaimed prophets (three women and one man) came on the scene. They didn't like Juanita at all, and decided to "expose" her for what they "thought" she really was. They started attacking her with all sorts of false accusations and lies. This was nothing more than a diabolical plot devised by Satan himself to destroy our "baby."

"She's a witch!"

"She's destroying this ministry."

"She's fake."

"She's not a true prophet."

"She doesn't hear from God; she hears from the demonic realm."

Juanita literally went through "hell." The bearers of those words fought hard against her anointing. They didn't realize they were fighting against God. She was the true prophet among them. As such, Juanita saw right through their attempts to silence her voice and extinguish God's call on her life. When their attacks finally culminated into an outright showdown, the ugliness of the matter came to light. I was well aware of who Juanita was, but wasn't completely certain that she was secure in the knowledge of her calling. So...I felt a confrontation was necessary for her to recognize who she really was and the authority she commanded in the Spirit.

> **I felt a confrontation was necessary for her to recognize who she really was and the authority she commanded in the Spirit.**

The "accusers" asked to meet with Juanita under the guise of "speaking" with her (i.e., not confronting), and she accepted. Then one unforgettable afternoon, the meeting took place in my office at the church. Not all of them showed up. That day, there were three pitted against one—Juanita was in the defensive position. This confrontation was reminiscent to Elijah's battle against Jezebel's prophets of Baal (see 1 Kings 18:17–40). I wasn't worried. In fact, I had encouraged my husband to let Juanita handle the situation. Spiritually, I knew the woman that she was...I was confident that she would rise up and discover she was fully capable of standing her ground. This "baby" had lived in my womb for some time—I felt that I knew her intricately.

I stood just outside the door as the accusations began to hurl. Juanita stood her ground. They were determined to prove she was a witch. All the while, she kept her composure and stepped into her anointing: *the office of a prophet.* What actually took place is they were *stunned* by her wisdom and *shaken* by her resolve and focus. They grew angrier by the moment...and the demons behind their attack began to surface.

Stubbornly, they refused to let up, and the battle began to tire her. So I entered the office and rebuked the accusers before asking them to leave the premises. They had no other choice but to obey.

Juanita was so angry; all she could do was cry. As I embraced her, God used me to administer the healing balm (of love) to her wounded soul before infection could set in. That's when she knew God had intervened. Once again, He was looking out for her; protecting her spirit from being completely broken.

I believe God allowed this partial breaking in her spirit in order to expose the part of her that still rebelled against Him at times, not allowing her to obey completely. Truly, though Juanita had come a long way in the things of God, she didn't always want to submit to His will. There were still areas where she was trying to live on the "border" of obedience. This half-heartedness was unacceptable to God; He had great plans for Juanita. Ultimately, she had to complete her *"death walk."*

That brokenness of spirit is what led Juanita into her destiny, beyond anything William or I had imagined. Let me say that God wants to do this with all of His children. He wants to take us beyond the surface into the depths and dimensions that only *death to self* can bring. It won't come any other way. If we fully submit unto God, our end will *always* be better than our beginning. This was evident in Juanita's life...even when she had to confront the forces that were trying to destroy her—especially those that were once within her soul.

Yes, this "showdown" was necessary for her spiritual development. Not only did Juanita need to prove her call to herself, but also to those who doubted. Juanita was powerful and mighty through God. And whether she realized it or not, she gave me strength as I carried her in my womb. I

> **Juanita was powerful and mighty through God. We had to let her feel some of the pain... without constant assistance and intervention.**

knew she didn't yet realize just how powerful and influential she was in God. So with this in mind, we had to let her *feel some of the pain* and go through some of the pressures without constant assistance and intervention.

Juanita saw herself as a fighter. This "baby" was no weakling. She wasn't about to let warfare snatch her from the womb. She couldn't afford to let false accusations take her out—so she fought back for the sake of her own future and self-esteem.

Today, those who accused her of deception are no longer operating in their "so-called" prophetic ministries. Their mouths were shut. All of them are struggling and have suffered tremendous loss as a result of "setting their mouths against" a prophet of God. Psalm 105:15 says that God reproved kings for the sake of His prophets, "...*Touch not mine anointed, and do my prophets no harm.*" We would do well to heed this word of wisdom today.

God has every intention of covering the ones He calls to be His voice in the earth.

I am inclined to believe God meant exactly what He said. He has every intention of covering the ones He calls to be His voice in the earth. True prophets will always be protected and vindicated by God.

You may have been thinking as you read, *If they truly loved her, how could they have allowed her to endure such persecution? Why did they allow such a direct attack on their daughter—perhaps scarring her for life?*

The answer lies in the reality that Juanita questioned her call and needed to know God was truly with her. She was frustrated by the struggle with her own spiritual identity. In other words, she needed to know that she was more than just "gifted." She also had to understand that she had authority in God, and that He was counting on her to withstand the test. (Sometimes, the best way to recognize and understand who we "are" is to be confronted with who we "are not.") Like dross is separated from pure gold "in the fire," so are our weaknesses when persecutions tap our true character in God. If we don't go into the "furnace of affliction," we can never be purified...

Like dross is separated from pure gold "in the fire," so are our weaknesses when persecutions tap our true character in God.

> So that [the genuineness] of your faith may be tested, [your faith] which is infinitely more precious than the perishable gold which is tested *and* purified by fire. [This proving of your faith is intended] to redound to [your] praise and glory and honor when Jesus Christ (the Messiah, the Anointed One) is revealed.
> —*1 Peter 1:7 AMPL*

This whole situation had been a divine "set up," designed by "Daddy God" with Juanita's spiritual development in mind. It was an opportunity for her to demonstrate the fruits of her true identity. When the accusers confronted Juanita and backed her into a corner, she came out swinging like the warrior God intended her to be. Juanita wasn't a passive little girl. She was a supernatural woman deep within. What's more, she had a destiny to *"glorify God"*—she was becoming a true ambassador for Christ by taking a stand and upholding His Word against strong resistance.

After that battle, the saints at New Hope developed a new level of respect for Juanita. She was the "last woman standing," her head held high with a new determination. On that day, I believe she became aware (more than ever) of who she was meant to be in the earth. *There's nothing like knowing who you are...and others recognizing it too.* Acknowledging your true spiritual identity is a sign of maturity and breakthrough in the things of God. It's a time when everything in your being awakens to your destiny. And this realization will keep you "alive" and "focused" in the face of many persecutions and afflictions. When you know who you are in Christ, nothing else really matters—because now, you can fulfill what you *know* from the depths of your being is your spiritual assignment.

Juanita warred well that day; there was a humility and Christ-likeness that rose up in her spirit. I believe that was the day she saw God's strength being "made perfect" in her weakness (see 2 Corinthians 12:7–10). Christ shined through Juanita like never before. Her accusers railed with insinuations, but she consistently responded back with the truth of God. Juanita gave them what God had given her

> **Juanita warred well that day; there was a humility and Christ-likeness that rose up in her spirit.**

and killed them with loving-kindness. Had she not waged this type of warfare, she wouldn't have endured this raging storm.

When the enemy came against her like a flood, the Spirit of the Lord raised a standard against it according to Isaiah 59:19. That day, torrential winds tried to tear Juanita away from her place in God, because the enemy wanted to drive her out of the womb—where she would be fully exposed, once again, to his evil devices. This didn't happen. As a proud mother, I can gladly say that she stood her ground and according to Hebrews 10:23, refused to let go of her "confession of faith." I remember it like it was yesterday...even if others deny it or have chosen to forget.

I thank God for His mercy. And beyond this, I thank Him for all of the issues that helped to shape Juanita into the woman she is today. As painful as it was for her at times, God has cleansed these memories and shown us the "big picture." The woman that had to endure horrendous accusations and persecutions "yesterday" has become a "weapon of power" *and* purpose for the kingdom of God.

Reflection and Study

1) Have you allowed your spiritual son or daughter to withstand attempted "womb assassinations" without intervening on his or her behalf? What happened? Recount the experience(s).

2) How was your protégé able to fully recover from these attacks?

3) Describe how these persecutions led to godly brokenness. Were you able to resist becoming offended on behalf of your spiritual offspring? How did God minister to your weakness?

4) Has your "baby" come into a full understanding of who he or she is in Christ as a result of these events? How do you know for sure?

5) What happened to the accusers? Has leadership dealt with these situations, or were the accusers never reproved? If not, what took place as a result? What do you think needs to be done for this confrontation to come full circle?

6) Is your child more focused on his or her spiritual assignment today than before these persecutions? What has demonstrated this to you?

7) Has the anointing that rests on your "spiritual baby's" life been raised to a new level as a result of acknowledging God's workings in his or her life? What supernatural fruit have you seen?

To the Prophet-in-the-Making

In embracing your divine charge, are you
learning to cleave unto God and let Him
defend and vindicate you?
Study 1 Kings 18

8

Spiritual Abortion...Destiny at Risk

Everything has already been decided. It was known long ago
what each person would be. So there's no use
arguing with God about your destiny.
—*Ecclesiastes 6:10 NLT*

In the Birth Canal

Nine years is a great length of time to invest in someone's life. After years of spiritual development, we longed to see Juanita come into the fullness of her potential in Christ. Yet, many outside forces were still working against her. The distraction of relationships was one of her biggest enemies. Juanita desperately wanted to be married again. Naturally, we understood her desire...but more than anything, we truly wanted God's will to be done. We hated it when she'd get pulled back into distraction right when she was on the verge of reaching a pivotal point in her spiritual development.

Juanita would open the door to her heart, and the enemy would use it to interrupt her focus. This happened too often. By nature, Juanita has always been very passionate. As a result, she always had a tendency to fall quick and hard for a man, losing herself in the relationship.

If she were to pursue another relationship, it could disturb the new freedom she'd gained through deliverance.

This was one area she had yet to yield fully unto God, and many times it had caused her to lose ground in the Spirit. We knew Juanita was in an extremely delicate phase of her development; she couldn't afford to lose her focus. If she were to pursue another relationship, it could cause old issues to arise and disturb the new freedom she'd gained through deliverance. So whenever those old waste products resurfaced within the "womb," it became Juanita's responsibility to excrete these relational issues and prevent them from poisoning her system. (Remember, when the time for "natural" birthing has come, a baby's system starts working on its own...even before the child is birthed out of its mother's womb.)

When Juanita didn't allow her system to expel this area of iniquity, our "baby" would begin to recede back into the womb. Instead of staying in the position to be birthed, she'd retreat from the pressure of the birth canal. She'd begin to "drop" into position and then lose focus...only to end up struggling against her own purpose and destiny, and going back to where she began.

Unlike pregnancy in the natural realm, spiritual birthing doesn't have a "due date." In the physical realm, parents are given a due date to prepare them for the arrival of their child. William and I weren't sure exactly when Juanita would come forth, but we knew she was closer than ever. And whether we realized it or not, God wanted Juanita to become so uncomfortable that she couldn't stay in the womb much longer. We loved her so much that if she had stayed exactly where she was, we would have continued to cover and care for her.

William and I weren't sure exactly when Juanita would come forth, but we knew she was closer than ever.

Later, we realized if she had remained in the womb, we could have gone past our grace. Then the "baby" would have been overdue. Juanita would have grown too large for the "womb," and the sac could have been ruptured beyond repair...risking death to both mother and child. As far as our daughter was concerned, this could have easily happened. Emotional soul ties were binding us together.

It's almost impossible for a mentor not to become tied to the soul of his or her protégé, because it's such a "close" experience. The same is true in a natural pregnancy; mother and baby are wholly connected in ways that cannot be defined…and it pierces all the way to blood, bone, and spirit. The mother feels everything the child feels in the physical realm, and likewise, the child experiences all of the mother's feelings on an emotional level. Mother and child are truly connected for life.

Certainly, a child is dependent upon its mother for survival. However, this can be dangerous; one can easily lose sight of the purpose for this coupling. The purpose of gestation isn't for the child to stay in the womb forever—but to come forth.

God was giving us wisdom and grace to know when Juanita was ready to leave. We knew her time in my spiritual womb was drawing to a close; but still, it wasn't *quite* time yet.

> **We knew her time in my spiritual womb was drawing to a close; but still, it wasn't quite time yet.**

The enemy was busy trying to cause "false labor" pangs, despite what we knew to be true. These "false contractions" were merely Satan's attempt to eject Juanita from the womb before God had given the word for her to be birthed. They were specifically assigned to push her out of the haven of security.

Juanita attempted many times to release herself before my water could break, which caused spiritual "leakage." Then God Himself had to counteract these attempts by "sewing up the womb" to prevent her untimely escape. Every time her struggles and pressures intensified, Juanita would struggle against the supernatural protection God had given her. She'd try to break free from the "spiritual incubator" that was sustaining her life.

Sometimes, a baby can appear to be fully formed (outwardly), but inwardly its lungs may not be strong enough to maintain consistent airflow. Without breath, there's no life. So the child needs to stay in the womb a bit longer before being presented to the outside world. Premature babies are only taken from their mothers when it's physically impossible for the pregnancy to continue. When these babies enter the world, they're immediately placed inside of an artificial incubator—an environment where their lungs can be closely monitored and protected as they develop to maturity.

During my false labor pangs, it was apparent that Juanita's "lungs" were not completely developed. Spiritually, she wasn't ready to live on her own...yet that still didn't stop her from trying to leave.

Spiritually, she wasn't ready to live on her own...yet that still didn't stop her from trying to leave.

For example, one Sunday (while Juanita was still living with us), she decided not to go to church with the rest of the family. So we went without her. After church, however, we returned to pick her up for dinner. (It was customary for us to eat together on Sunday.) When we arrived at the house, we sent one of our children inside to let Juanita know we were waiting for her to go out with us. She adamantly refused the invitation.

Juanita had already packed her bags and was preparing to leave for the train station. Her intense refusal encouraged my husband to go inside. When he entered the house, he confronted her. I was curious about what he was going to say to Juanita, so I followed closely behind.

With all her belongings packed, she appeared to be so sure of herself. Juanita truly thought she could stand her ground without being moved. That's when her "spiritual father" told her she *was* going to dinner with the rest of us, and when we got back, she was going to unpack her things. She wasn't going anywhere. Juanita was shocked…but because she was willing to honor the man of God and walk in obedience to her spiritual leaders, she didn't disrespect him. Immediately, she got herself together and headed to the car.

God knew Juanita needed that kind of authority and discipline in her life. She'd come a long way, but she hadn't come far enough to determine when her birthing would take place—any more than an unborn infant could declare the exact moment it would be birthed from the physical womb. It would happen in God's timing…if Juanita would stay obedient to His voice.

God determines when a child is to emerge from the womb. He ordains the pangs and the process of pushing. So in

> **God determines when a child is to emerge from the womb.**

His perfect timing, Juanita's birthing process wouldn't be interrupted. Nothing would prevent this "spiritual baby" from emerging into the world.

Breaking the Tie of the Soul

The umbilical cord between Juanita and me represented an intense connection in the Spirit realm during her time of gestation. It was so deeply embedded that when she needed to be birthed, it wouldn't release its function over to Juanita's system. Therefore, God knew something outside of Juanita and me—something far stronger than either one of us—had to sever our souls. In other words, God had to separate us.

During this time, Juanita suffered intervals of "trauma" that caused her to feel she'd been lost in the connection; times that I wasn't able to be there for her when she needed me. (Bear in mind, I was also dealing with tremendous strain in my own life. I was struggling through my own inner battles during this spiritual pregnancy.) Sometimes my husband, biological children, and extended family members couldn't fully understand the internal issues I was dealing with. And when I was hit the hardest, my family suffered loss, along with the "daughter" I was carrying in the Spirit.

God had to separate us.

Added to this, I was nearing the end of my pregnancy and I was emotionally, spiritually, mentally, and physically wiped out. This was also a very difficult time for Juanita. It bruised and wounded her deeply when she'd try to reach out to me, and I was too drained to reach back.

Juanita began to struggle again with knowing and feeling confident in her spiritual identity—and the biggest area of struggle was in the area of functioning in her calling. At times, she honestly didn't want any part of being a prophetess. She wanted to be left alone to live a "normal" life. However, God wasn't about to leave Juanita to her own determinations, no matter how she kicked and screamed against the process. Like I said before, until we reached this stage of my pregnancy, Juanita always knew she could rely on me. But in the heat of the process, suddenly, she felt completely isolated.

Juanita began to struggle again with knowing and feeling confident in her spiritual identity.

The battles of this prophetess-in-the-making were enormous. She desperately wanted to escape, but the God of her creation was relentless in His pursuit.

In my time of weakness, God used others to strengthen her—particularly my family. Our oldest daughter, Cherise, really hung in there with Juanita. She understood her sister's struggles, because she also has a prophetic call on her life.

Bridgette, our youngest, was an intercessor for Juanita—always using the Word of God when she needed to relay a message to her. During rough periods, she'd bring scriptures to Juanita, even when she had no desire to receive them. It didn't matter to Bridgette; she'd speak God's truth, no matter what.

There were moments when my spiritual daughter didn't understand me, especially toward the end of the pregnancy. (Later, I realized her sense of being lost may have been her actual "contractions," even though no one was aware of it at the time.) Perhaps these awkward times were necessary, representing the "waters" of my womb beginning to break. Yet, just as natural babies may experience a feeling of confusion in the womb when this haven (they've been growing in for nine months) starts to become inhospitable; Juanita may not have understood what was really happening, either. And at the time, we weren't aware of this.

Pre-Term Labor

> Jezebel always desires to kill the prophet.

In addition, a person who was operating under the spirit of Jezebel spoke heartbreaking words to Juanita. No one was able to prevent the damage they'd ultimately cause...Jezebel always desires to kill the prophet (see 1 Kings 19:1–2). This person nearly succeeded.

This was the first sign of pre-term labor. My spiritual cervix was beginning to thin, shorten, and soften for delivery. On top of this, there was so much stress in the womb, fluid began to leak out—first in a trickle and then in a gush—even though God had stitched the ruptures to keep Juanita there until her time was fulfilled. That person—*the voice of deception in her ears*—was pushing her farther away from her destiny.

The contractions, though irregular, were still reminding us that something was about to happen...*soon*. Our "baby," Juanita, became highly confused. We couldn't help wondering, *Is this the real moment she's supposed to come forth? Is she really supposed to be birthed this way?*

The deceptive words from the womb of Jezebel caused Juanita to experience a deeper sense of urgency; she felt she had no choice but to leave the womb. Juanita had internalized the lies that had been spoken...which caused a breach between mother and daughter.

> **Juanita felt she had no choice but to leave the womb.**

Then more contractions started coming, with much greater intensity, indicating that my "bones" were beginning to separate...we had no choice, the outcome was sure. The lies..."word curses"...were causing a premature birth. More than what had been spoken, this person had communicated in a way that Juanita presupposed the "lies" had come under the authority of my voice. This is what made her believe that she had to leave. Each contraction continued pushing her farther away from my protective haven.

Finally, intense contractions catapulted my "baby" from the "womb."

A Healthy Birth?

Juanita left Port Huron and returned to Chicago with all of her belongings...including the hurt she still carried in her heart. Suddenly, she was in a dark place. When the frigid air of the outside world hit her naked body, she cried and cried...her surroundings were no longer familiar. Juanita could no longer hear the loving voices of her parents encouraging her within the walls of the womb. She'd

> **Juanita left Port Huron and returned to Chicago with all of her belongings...including the hurt she still carried in her heart.**

experienced an abrupt detachment from her spiritual mother, and now, she was exposed to the elements. I could feel her spirit crying out, *How did I get here?* All Juanita could do was lay there, blinking in the light...trying desperately to get her bearings.

Her birthing hadn't been a blissful awakening; a beautiful breaking forth. Instead, it had been a violent burst of blood, water, and mucus. It had brought pain and hurt, instead of release. And it had left Juanita with an unhealthy fear of the unknown...and, a profound sense of betrayal.

Amazingly, due to the most unlikely of circumstances, when Juanita emerged she was still connected in the Spirit. Yes, the umbilical cord was still attached; it hadn't yet been completely severed because she

> **The Great Physician hadn't "cut" our spiritual attachment...Juanita contacted us again.**

had been birthed before God's ordained timing. The Great Physician hadn't "cut" our spiritual attachment. This was quite unlike the procedure usually applied in a natural birth process; the cord is cut as soon as the baby is born, so the child can begin living and functioning on its own.

Juanita contacted us again, but it wasn't before the enemy managed to wreak havoc in her life. Some of the strongholds she'd been delivered from had begun to re-attach themselves. She was afraid because she knew this wasn't her lifestyle any longer—*something was seriously wrong.* She called my husband and repented for leaving prematurely. Once she re-connected with us and received our covering again, it was as if the light of God literally drove out the darkness. Again, she was freed from the bondage of Satan's vice. And even though she didn't return to Port Huron, she continued to speak with us concerning her life...until she joined the church she currently attends in New York.

> **Even outside of the "womb," Juanita was able to complete the birthing process.**

God was merciful. Even outside of the "womb," Juanita was able to complete the birthing process. Slowly but surely, she began to move and live on her own. And then finally...the cord was cut and the placenta was detached from the walls deep within my spirit.

Juanita's departure was another divine "set-up," which I didn't realize until the writing of this book. Due to all of the false labor, my husband and I had concluded that the enemy succeeded in driving her out. For a long time, I contemplated my daughter's "untimely birth." Yet, I wasn't completely satisfied that God hadn't succeeded in bringing forth the plan He'd ordained from the beginning.

When Juanita left, it was hard on all of us. There were so many unanswered questions. Something just wasn't right. We didn't learn right away that when Juanita felt the first contraction...the first sensation...that she was about to be pushed out. Later—long after she'd come into her own as a prophetess to the nations—she revealed to me what had been spoken (this was approximately six years ago).

After Juanita shared this with me, I couldn't believe such intense pain could ever be part of a spiritual birthing. I was deeply hurt by the lies that had been spoken to her; they had infiltrated my "womb" without me even knowing it.

However...the revelation ultimately came that God had allowed it—not for our hurt, but to bring about a bigger plan. If those "word curses" hadn't been spoken, our "baby" wouldn't have been put in the necessary position for birthing. God used that traumatic situation to keep Juanita on the course of destiny. To our dismay, she endured more pain and trials upon her return to Chicago. We continued praying for her, covering her until the time came for God to place her in the care of a Pastor who could "water" her and nurture the seeds we'd planted.

> **God had allowed it—not for our hurt, but to bring about a bigger plan.**

I came to realize that if those Braxton-Hicks contractions hadn't forced Juanita out of the "womb," we wouldn't have required her to leave my protective haven. This would have been even more dangerous—because if you delay what God has ordained to happen (as I stated before), the spiritual ramifications could be fatal.

> **If you delay what God has ordained to happen, the spiritual ramifications could be fatal.**

Ultimately, Juanita had to leave our care...one way or the other. Perhaps she had left a little too soon, but God was undaunted by the enemy's deception. He was still going to have His way.

Juanita couldn't afford to continue her life in the womb, because an array of demonic spirits had been released against us: witchcraft, jealousy, and deceit topped the list. God saw the impending onslaught of the enemy and allowed Juanita to be released. He knew that otherwise, she'd end up repeatedly reliving past mistakes...and that just couldn't happen. Juanita had come so far in Christ; the cost of reverting to old behaviors would have been too high. She had obediently invested much into her destiny. Those destructive spirits would have caused a partial-birth abortion. In other words, Juanita would have come out of the womb just far enough to have her life aborted before she could be fully birthed.

> **Juanita had come so far in Christ; the cost of reverting to old behaviors would have been too high.**

Once in Chicago, Jezebel's destructive force went back to work on Juanita—trying to kill the prophetess she was meant to become by disgracing and scandalizing her identity. Yet, the grace and mercy of God intervened and prevented any further harm to His anointed vessel.

> **God reminded me that His purpose wasn't for her to "die," but according to Psalm 118:17, to live and declare the works of the Lord.**

All the while (until she clarified it with me years later), it appeared to Juanita that the woman who had once carried and taken care of her, had actually turned against her. My womb, once a place of refuge and haven, had suddenly become a den of rejection— bringing such pain to Juanita that she had to leave. And though Jezebel's accusations were indeed "lies," God still allowed Juanita's sudden departure. He ejected her from my womb, protecting her as she went along her way. God reminded me that His purpose wasn't for her to "die," but according to Psalm 118:17, to *live and declare the works of the Lord.*

God had every intention of seeing Juanita grow well beyond her gestational period. She would go forth boldly to the nations. We couldn't hold onto Juanita any longer. If we had, we would have been in danger of stepping beyond the realms of grace. We had to accept that we'd only been given a certain amount of grace to carry our "baby." Trying to go beyond that boundary would have been disastrous...for all of us. Juanita wouldn't have continued on the path God had set before her, and we wouldn't have been able to continue bringing forth our spiritual lineage.

A New Spiritual Seed

Later, God planted a "son" in my "womb" that had a kindred anointing and calling. Timothy Alden came into our lives, and lived in our home for three years. During that time, we re-instituted the lessons we'd learned from our "firstborn." While it didn't take nearly as long to birth Timothy, we applied the same amount of loving care to catapult this young man to his next level in God. He was very much like Juanita; he carried the call of the prophet within. Actually, they're almost twins in the Spirit. Anyone who experiences Timothy's ministry has said it's obvious he and Juanita came from the same "spiritual parents."

With Timothy, we made sure he went through the appointed time for his deliverance. Certainly, we didn't want any "blockages" hindering his growth, because we remembered how important the "spiritual freedom" of sustained deliverance is to the prophetic call. We knew that he, too, was called to the nations and had to be totally prepared for the vision God had placed before him. God had need of Timothy, Juanita, and other spiritual children to come—so He kept encouraging us in our call. He couldn't allow the enemy to resurface any "wastes" from our past. He wanted His children to live, not to be killed before their time. Every prophet-in-the-making has an appointment with destiny...but it takes vessels who are *willing* and *obedient* to birth them out.

Now, Timothy flows in the prophetic vein and also pastors a church in California. He's a very powerful man of God in his own right, and is used mightily by the Lord in the lives of young people.

William and I are proud of our spiritual children. We're so glad that "freedom" ultimately came for them both. Now, this same freedom is extending into the lives of others—affecting communities, cities, and of course...the nations. For both of them, the time of birthing was crucial and necessary. We never took it lightly! Today, as my husband and I become parents to more men and women of God, we continue to embrace deliverance as a vital part of our ministry.

Reflection and Study

1) What did you and your "baby" experience when the time of birthing came? Were you ready to release your child from the womb, or did God have to perform a divine ejection?

2) Describe that experience, with the insights you've now received from God.

3) Did you experience an encounter with Jezebel in the final stages of gestation, or at any time during your spiritual pregnancy? Take a moment to identify her strategy and method(s). If you haven't done it already, break those strongholds off of your life, and that of your spiritual offspring, for good...by the power of the Blood of Jesus!

4) How did you become "weary" in the final stages of your third trimester in the Spirit? How did your family become involved?

5) When did the "real contractions" begin? What set them off...spiritually, and in the natural?

6) Describe any "confusion" that you perceived (or were later told) your child was experiencing in the womb...just before birthing came.

7) Is he or she still under your spiritual oversight, or have you released this child into the care of another? Recount that experience in light of seeing God's prophetic plan come to pass.

To the Prophet-in-the-Making

Are you learning to discern the subtle devices of the enemy
that are trying to abort your purpose in God? Is God birthing
you out, or are you trying to deliver yourself?

Study 1 Kings 19

The Bitter Cup

...O my Father, if it be possible, let this cup pass from me:
nevertheless not as I will, but as thou *wilt*....O my Father, if this cup
may not pass away from me, except I drink it, thy will be done.
—*Matthew 26:39, 42*

You may be wondering how this scripture relates to spiritual pregnancy and the birthing of prophets. Let me explain the revelation of "pregnancy." It deals with the idea of connection, oneness, and the knitting together of souls. It invokes the reality of how one soul is dependent upon another. During a pregnancy, spiritual or natural, the baby is in a state of pure and utter dependence upon the mother. They are truly one...until birthing and separation take place.

Pregnancy also points to the correlating relationship between God the Father and Jesus, His Son. During my years of ministry, I can recall hearing the Father—*El Shaddai*—being referred to as the "All-Breasted One." This term reflects deep intimacy...*they were inseparable.* Jesus was totally dependent upon the Father, just as a growing fetus depends on his mother to survive.

Now, let's move on. Like a natural pregnancy, some developmental elements must take place outside of the "spiritual womb." Growth doesn't end with the birthing process. When a child is separated from the haven of its mother, he or she must encounter and overcome the "external"

> **Jesus had to be separated from His Father...His ultimate Source of life and strength.**

enemies of abundant life. Think of it this way. Jesus had to be separated from His Father in heaven, His ultimate Source of life and strength. So He had to die to self in Gethsemane before He could endure "physical death" at Calvary.

In His confrontation with eternal destiny, Jesus realized that He had lost His "connection" with His Father (see Matthew 27:46). To fulfill the will of God, it had been severed. The divine umbilical cord had to be "cut" as the sins of the world were placed upon Him—because the Father couldn't look upon sin. Jesus exchanged an eternity of intimate fellowship with the Father for unbearable pain and darkness. Yet, to fulfill the living Word of God, Jesus willingly severed Himself from His Source of life and strength.

I believe Jesus' greatest fear wasn't of "death," but rather, the fear of "separation." He had to contend with fear in order to fulfill His destiny. *Does this sound familiar?* Most

> **Jesus' greatest fear wasn't of "death," but rather, the fear of "separation."**

importantly, a lost and dying world was at stake...so the warfare was intense. Jesus was a Son, but He was also a mighty prophet...and like a baby inside a mother's womb...He'd never been separated from the One Who'd given Him divine utterance. He'd been with God from the beginning. All things existed because they were one (see John 1:1–3, Colossians 1:12–17). Suddenly, He was alone.

God's purpose for Jesus was to drink this "bitter cup"—His ultimate step of obedience. *What if He'd decided not to do it? What if He'd decided it wasn't worth being separated from the Father?* Yes...He would have forfeited the destiny and redemption of all mankind. This would have been far worse than "spiritual abortion," it would have been genocide. For this reason, Jesus had to die, *sweating great drops of blood*, even before He went to the cross. To the extent He was destined to be used by the Father, Jesus had to die to self.

At some point, every servant of God must do the same. For a prophet-in-the-making, every drop of this "cup" must be consumed, no matter how bitter or humiliating it may be. Our Savior faced a tragic separation from His Heavenly Father on Calvary. He struggled through the dark night of His soul, warring against His own emotions. And just as Christ came through this dark time of separation, so must we if we are going to do His work.

> **To the extent He was destined to be used by the Father, Jesus had to die to self.**

Killing the Spirit of Rejection

Throughout His struggle in Gethsemane, Jesus desired that *someone* would help Him bear the pain. He asked His disciples to undergird Him in intercession...but they couldn't even stay awake. This is akin to the prophet's solitary experience. He or she must come to a place and time when potentially supportive people cannot give needed aid because of their own weaknesses. What must a true prophet do? We must drink the bitter cup.

Perhaps the harshest element of Jesus' battle that ended at Calvary was encountering the spirit of rejection. Inevitably, every prophet must face this enemy. Rejection is a mighty foe. For example, I can still hear the deceptive words of that foul spirit in my ear, telling me that my spiritual daughter would never return to me...that our fellowship was severed forever. *The devil is a liar!* Since we both operate in the office of a prophet, he launched an

> **A true prophet must drink the bitter cup.**

attack that was twice as lethal—not just to bring down a prophet, but to extinguish a spiritual legacy. Thanks be to God, he didn't succeed.

I can just hear him saying, "Leave that alone! Keep quiet! I don't want people to know that I'm really the most diabolical spirit of all. I am the spirit that can stop kings, rulers, and great leaders, the rich and the poor, the educated and the illiterate, believers in God and nonbelievers alike. I am shrewd and unnoticed unless my enemy, the Holy Spirit, exposes me to those who are yielded to and controlled by Him—those who know how to hear and listen to God's voice and follow His unction."

As saints and believers, we can praise God that our Savior Jesus Christ overcame the "spirit of rejection" through prayer and by humbly submitting Himself to the Father's will. His victory ensures ours. Jesus prayed in the Garden of Gethsemane and came to the place of self-surrender and complete humility. He came into His Father's presence and received the strength to endure the ultimate "separation." Yes, Jesus was "pressed out" like an olive on an oil press...but the anointing of the Holy Spirit overshadowed Him, bringing final victory over rejection and death.

As a people of God, and His prophets, I believe our lives must be "pressed out" (in our own Garden of Gethsemane) so that we can be anointed for destiny and purpose. There's no other way around it. Every great man or woman of God has had to travel this route. Throughout the ages, prophets (and others that were greatly used of God) had to go through *Gethsemane*. Most importantly, Jesus—our forerunner, predecessor, and

> **Juanita had to take this same walk of darkness, rejection, and death before being "totally delivered" into her destiny.**

the author and finisher of our faith—followed this path in order to embrace His ultimate purpose.

Juanita had to embrace this reality. She had to take this same walk of darkness, rejection, and death before being "totally delivered" into her destiny. And thanks be to God, she endured to the end. Every prophet-in-the-making has to follow a unique path and drink his or her own "bitter cup." Juanita's course had been "chiseled out" for *her alone*. And these experiences birthed her destiny in God. If you surrender unto God in Gethsemane, so will yours.

There is a cost to fulfilling your divine destiny, and that's why fear tries to make you seek out a way of escape. Watch out. Fear will paralyze you. It is a destiny-breaker. So no matter what, don't listen to fear or follow your "natural" emotions. You'll stay on the course God has set before you, even when God requires that you walk alone.

> **Fear is a destiny-breaker.**

In another way, Juanita's experience wasn't unique. She went to Gethsemane *alone* and *afraid*—much like Jesus did. She had been delivered, albeit prematurely, from the safety and protection of the "womb," only to face the greatest battle of her life. Thank God, by this point, she had already learned that her calling was too precious to risk abandoning or losing it altogether.

> **Juanita could not avoid enduring her own "dark night of the soul."**

Juanita could not, and ultimately would not, avoid enduring her own "dark night of the soul." She had to face herself and the final stand of the enemy before her deliverance could be fully released. Once and for all, she had to move beyond her feelings and emotions—*sins of the soul that had easily beset her*—like constantly wondering how God could possibly want to use her, or thinking that other people with "more capabilities" were of far greater value to God. And finally, Juanita had to face and master the most lethal of all her inner enemies: self-pity and self-rejection.

Then there were the rejections, which came from "outside" during this time. When others rejected her, Juanita just wanted to give up and leave it all behind. Some of her deepest hurts came either when people of great renown, or her family and friends (whom she expected to protect and understand her) did just the opposite. Like Jesus, when she needed them most, people couldn't take this death walk with her. This was ordained of God.

> **Like Jesus, when she needed them most, people couldn't take this death walk with her.**

Eventually, after a grueling struggle *within* and *without*, Juanita resigned herself to the fact that no matter what, she had to drink the "bitter cup." Juanita went into Gethsemane and learned the true power of prayer. She tapped into principles she had gleaned from her prayer mentors. The only way she could endure and submit unto the Father was by learning to pray like Jesus prayed—until God's desires became her own, "...O my Father, if this cup may not pass from me, except I drink it, thy will be done" (Matthew 26:42). All along, this is what the Father desired...complete obedience and humility. Her "bitter cup," which had been emptied out, was filled once again.

Juanita realized she could no longer expect others to join her on this "death walk" or drink her "bitter cup." This was between her and God alone. Because during this process, He was establishing a covenant with Juanita...He was taking her to a new level in the Spirit realm. And He was "jealous" for her to finally make a total commitment to Him.

God told her: "Drink my Blood or you will have no part with Me."

As Juanita partook of the shed Blood of Jesus, she realized the pain, suffering, and distress of all the people whose lives she'd eventually touch were part of this "dark night of the soul." Yes...the worldwide ministry God had prepared for her was in that "bitter cup." Therefore, it was time for death to become "complete"—because nations were hanging in the balance.

> **The worldwide ministry God had prepared for her was in that "bitter cup."**

The Final Victory

Gagging on its contents, Juanita finally swallowed every drop from the "bitter cup." But first, she had to be willing to pick it up—and that was as much a struggle as drinking it. Why? It opened the door for her to confront her greatest struggle of all...the test she had failed so many times before...*her tendency to fall into sexual sin.* At this point, Juanita had overcome every other battle. And though she knew it would be painful, she refused to be taken down by this stronghold. Juanita opened her heart in total submission to the Father's will and poured herself out unto death. Finally, her deliverance was complete.

When she wrote *No More Sheets*, her personal deliverance was released to the world. Thousands have now been delivered from sexual bondage to the glory of God!

As I said before, Juanita was truthful in terms of her struggle. Thankfully, I can say that she never lied to me when she had fallen into sin, finding herself entangled in another ungodly relationship. Her ability to confess (in obedience to God) was really the first step toward total deliverance...and the same is true for you. Juanita wouldn't hide her sin or pain from her spiritual authority, which is a key ingredient in any mentoring relationship. You must be truthful with those who "watch out for your soul" to stay connected to your destiny. God desires truth in the inward parts—in your heart—no matter how difficult this may be. So no matter what's in your "bitter cup," it's time to drink every drop. It's time for you to receive total deliverance so that you can go to your next level in God. Souls are at stake.

As Juanita's spiritual mother, I was able to see into her life with clarity. God gave me this insight for her own good. For instance, one Sunday after church God showed me that Juanita had been sexually active the night before. I confronted her with that revelation and she confessed it was true. Although it seemed that her constant confession was "cyclical," it was necessary to her development. Her confessions made the enemy's attempts to secretly infiltrate her life ineffective. And they helped her to see this "sin" for what it really was—a separation from her destiny. Juanita knew she'd have to obey the voice of God or risk destruction by continuing to walk on this path that was outside of His plan for her life.

Once Juanita crossed over into total obedience, she never turned back. She stayed on course and let the contents of this "cup" fill her mind, body, and spirit. Juanita was transformed into a totally different woman. Fear no longer had a foothold in her life. The Blood of Christ had prevailed! It broke the power of this stronghold for good and invoked the power of obedience—catapulting Juanita to a new level in God. This time, Juanita gave herself to Him fully. She was no

Once Juanita crossed over into total obedience, she never turned back.

longer "partially betrothed" to the Lord, still embracing old patterns of sin and iniquity.

And, no, Juanita didn't become a Superwoman. She humbled herself, tapped into the power of a *supernatural God*, and started experiencing Holy Spirit power like never before. At last, Juanita had embraced her destiny! Finally, she'd allowed herself to endure the process of complete brokenness. And even though Gethsemane would prove to be the beginning of Juanita's deeper battles (on her next level in the Spirit realm), she endured and overcame strongholds from her past as she "pressed in" to the place of prayer. At last, Juanita's breakthrough had come. The spiritual birthing process was complete.

Today, Gethsemane is what keeps her alive. Total surrender keeps her moving forward in the purpose of God.

Are you willing to drink the cup?

Reflection and Study

1) How is your spiritual son or daughter enduring Gethsemane, the process of separation from your spiritual womb? List a few thoughts.

2) To the best of your ability, describe the contents you're able to see in your spiritual baby's "bitter cup." Then make intercession unto God.

3) What is your "bitter cup"? How has this time of separation affected you? Your natural family?

4) Can you see the spirit of rejection being broken off of your child's life and ministry? Is he or she seeing progress in this area?

5) What rejections have come? Do you think your spiritual son or daughter has come to the point of facing the "dark night of the soul"? Explain why or why not.

6) Describe this new level of "walking alone" in God, for you personally, and also what you've witnessed in the life of your spiritual offspring.

7) Through it all, have you (and your spiritual child) discovered the power of prayer in Gethsemane? List a few things that have revealed you are embarking upon a new level in God. How do you see ministry being renewed in both of your lives?

To the Prophet-in-the-Making

What is your "bitter cup"? Are you afraid to
confront your deepest fears in order to embrace
your destiny? Press into God and be free!

Study Matthew 26 and 27

Elijah's Mantle

Background Reading: 1 Kings 19 and 2 Kings 2

The prophet Elijah performed powerful and mighty exploits for God. Yet, behind the scenes (underneath it all), he was just a man who struggled with many weaknesses. Elijah battled constantly against depression, fear, and rejection. He wasn't popular or well liked; but he commanded respect because of the authority of the office he walked in.

The spirit of rejection, discussed in the last chapter, plagued Elijah. He warred with it more than any other spirit, and I believe that's why he was "alone" during most of his ministry. Time and again, Elijah was driven into isolation; unable to function well with others. This wasn't only due to the spirit of rejection, but also, the calling on his life gave a rough edge to his personality. Elijah was harsh, abrupt, and sometimes rude—but he knew his God, and his God knew him.

While Elijah had many "unseen" enemies, he also had an enemy in the natural realm that set herself against him— Queen Jezebel. She became an

> **Jezebel constantly threatened and intimidated the man of God.**

intimidating force in his life. And ultimately, he ran away trying to escape from her threats. Jezebel had the audacity to believe she was a match for God. (Of course, at the end of her tirade, she suffered an immeasurable defeat at the hand of God.)

Before this defeat, however, Jezebel constantly threatened and intimidated the man of God. You may remember from the Preface that when Elijah was wearied by her insults and threats, he ran away into the wilderness. He ended up lying down under the shade of a juniper tree—desiring to die. Shortly thereafter, in the midst of his humiliation, he entertained thoughts of suicide.

God never answered Elijah's request to die. Instead, He sent an angel to minister to Elijah's most immediate needs—food, drink, and strength. The angel commanded him to

God knew exactly what Elijah needed.

"arise and eat." In doing this, God showed that He didn't consider Elijah's depressed state of mind, even though He was concerned for his well-being. God knew exactly what Elijah needed.

After eating and drinking, Elijah laid back down. Then the angel of the Lord came back a second time and commanded him to eat, saying, "...the journey *is* too great for thee" (1 Kings 19:7). Perhaps the angel wasn't referring to his "physical" journey, but rather, the spiritual (inward) journey.

Again, Elijah obeyed. The food he ate sustained him supernaturally, "He...went in the strength of that meat forty days and forty nights unto Horeb the mount of God" (1 Kings 19:8). However, instead of recognizing God's hand of deliverance and protection, Elijah hid in a cave. Only then did God address his inner struggles:

> And he said, 'I have been very zealous for the Lord God of hosts because the children of Israel have forsaken Your covenant, torn down your altars, and killed Your prophets with the sword. I alone am left; and they seek to take my life.' Then the Lord said to him: Go, return on your way to the Wilderness of Damascus; and when you arrive, anoint Hazael as king over Syria. Also you shall anoint Jehu the son of Nimshi as king over Israel. And Elisha the son of

Shaphat of Abel Meholah you shall anoint as prophet in your place.

—*1 Kings 19:14-16*

Elijah obeyed the instructions of the Lord without further delay. When Elijah found Elisha, he was plowing a field with oxen; he threw his cloak over the young man to symbolize the call. I think the most powerful revelation of this story is Elisha recognized what it meant. In his response to Elijah, he demonstrated a complete understanding of his calling and selection. Elisha left everything—his family, livelihood, and any plans he'd made for his own future. Obediently, he chose to follow the man of God—to submit himself to life in

> **Elisha left everything—his family, livelihood, and any plans he'd made for his own future.**

the "womb." And he ended up "covering his feet" for many years. (In the Old Testament, this term poetically described becoming a servant to someone else.)

Elisha chose to stay in the womb until God removed Elijah from his earthly ministry. Imagine that. Elisha's gestational period lasted for years. When God selected Elisha, it didn't mean He intended for him to flow in the prophetic vein immediately. It meant that God wanted Elijah to train this young man to make an eternal impact when the time was right.

> **Submission to God-given authority is the crux of training for prophetic ministry.**

Again, the key to successful mentorship is submission—for the prophet Elisha, Juanita Bynum, or anyone else. I cannot emphasize this enough. Submission to God-given authority is the crux of training for prophetic ministry. A person cannot be trained without being submitted to the one who must lead him or her to the High Places in God. Always remember these important principles of ministry:

1) Submission for Service (unto God, your spiritual authorities, and others)

2) Servitude and Servanthood (the only way you can be fully prepared for ministry)

Submission: A Lifestyle

In layman's terms, *submission* means to yield to someone else's power or authority. In everything, we must first submit to the will of God. James 4:7 tells us to submit unto God, resist the devil...and he will flee from us. Submission kills the devil's devices.

Scripture also conveys the message that in order to obey the principle of submission, we must not only submit to God-given leadership, but also to each other as brothers and sisters in the Lord (see Ephesians 5:21). By living in submission, we become true reflections of Christ—the way to harmony and true freedom. Like I said before, submission is the key to spiritual deliverance. Every person on the earth desires harmony—within our own lives, with others, and with God. We all want to be "free indeed."

Complete submission plays a vital part in becoming whole, wholesome, and fulfilled (as in Elisha's walk with Elijah and Juanita's ultimate walk with me). When we learn to become obedient "for the Lord's sake," it strengthens our walk with God *and* our influence for His kingdom. So if you want to fulfill the mission and mandate of God in your life, you have to embrace total submission—be willing to give up your "right" to be "right." Humble yourself, even at the risk of losing face.

The reality of *submission* is you cannot become a minister of the Lord on your own. At some point, you'll have to submit to what you know is the will of the Lord, even if it means that you will be put into a state of obeisance unto another—a spiritual "father" or "mother." Your "father or mother in ministry" can train you to produce an effective and longstanding ministry. And this will inevitably release your true inheritance in Christ...the portion due to you as a "son" or

> **You cannot become a minister of the Lord on your own—a spiritual "father" or "mother" will inevitably release your true inheritance in Christ.**

"daughter" in Zion. Only true sons and daughters receive an inheritance, so you must be properly parented and validated by apostolic authority.

The blessing of God accompanies those who choose to submit. I'm sure that as Elisha served the prophet, he witnessed Elijah's personal struggles and issues. I'm also certain he helped the man of God walk through them. Elisha's presence in the prophet's life seemed to dismiss Elijah's

> **The blessing of God accompanies those who choose to submit.**

battle with depression, fear, and rejection—they were no longer mentioned in the scriptures.

Elijah's personality didn't change, but he adapted well in the role of father and mentor to Elisha. And Elisha, the prophet-in-the-making, fully accepted Elijah as a teacher, trainer, and instructor. He opened his heart and spirit to receive everything the old prophet could deposit inside of him. And he never thought of leaving Elijah...Elisha's love for his spiritual father compelled him to remain; not only as a servant, but a trusted companion.

Four Stages of Development

Elisha was trained for ministry by seeing first-hand accounts of the many great feats Elijah was graced to perform by the Spirit. He recognized Elijah's great ferocity for God. This "spiritual son" received everything he could during his years of service. Like a spiritual sponge, he absorbed knowledge, wisdom, and power from his mentor. Yes, Elisha obtained many "mantles" (i.e., anointings) from Elijah.

In order to receive his inheritance (i.e., Elijah's mantles), Elisha had to come through four distinct stages with his "father" and mentor.

> **Elisha had to come through four distinct stages...Gilgal, Bethel, Jericho, and Jordan.**

The first was **Gilgal**—where he learned to walk by faith and where the old "cycles of life" are broken. The second place was **Bethel**—where Elisha would learn to overcome tests, trials, and tribulations. **Jericho** was the place of war. It's where Satan himself wars against the man and woman of God. At this stage, one learns the art of war and how to defeat the enemy of the soul. This is also where the called of God take the "death walk." Finally, Elisha reached **Jordan**—where every gift from God was at his disposal. Here, he could ask for anything from God, and He supplied it according to His will.

After your faith is built in **Gilgal,** you overcome tests and trials in **Bethel,** and then encounter spiritual warfare and death to self in **Jericho.** Then, you become able to submit unto God in total obedience and unwavering commitment. Once you have endured all four stages, like Elisha did, God knows that He can trust you to carry out your destiny. And then...you enter **Jordan!**

As it was for Elisha, so will it be for every prophet-in-the-making. It can be agonizing to gain the victory in all of these areas; such is the "furnace of affliction." Notice that at the beginning of their relationship, it seemed that Elijah didn't want Elisha to pursue him any further. It was as though Elijah was intentionally trying to cause his "son" to miss the impartation and deposits he needed in order to fulfill his destiny and purpose.

In return, Elisha became dogmatic, which let Elijah know that he wouldn't leave until he'd received his inheritance as a son—his spiritual "birthright." Elisha had to put everything on the line. Everything he had and every part of who he was as a person was at stake. Yet, he pressed through and overcame every trial so that he could proceed on to his next level in God. Finally, Elisha had to war with Satan, battling him for destiny's sake. And beyond that, he had to die to himself (at his spiritual Gethsemane), relinquishing his will, desires, opinions, fears, and agendas.

> **Through it all, Elisha sold out to the perfect will of God.**

Through it all, Elisha sold out to the perfect will of God. Otherwise, he never would have obtained his inheritance. He had to make it through the "furnace of affliction" to receive the "double portion" from his spiritual father, Elijah. Above everything else, he received the ultimate mantle from Elijah...*the anointing of God.* Everything he'd known and seen in his "father" came to him with double power, double revelation, and the "double strength" of God flowing into him. Elijah's impartation produced a bountiful outcome—a doubly powerful man of God!

Don't get me wrong; I'm not trying to say that Elisha was trouble-free. He, too, faced personal issues and struggles, but he laid it all aside and served from the depths of his heart. The seeds of greatness were evident within Elisha. Yet he had to endure the final processes in order to gain his inheritance and go to the next level in God—because Elisha had to reach higher levels than Elijah was able to reach in his lifetime. It was his spiritual destiny.

Eventually, Elisha also learned how to mentor others. One day, he'd have to become a father to someone else who would continue in Elijah's legacy. And he wouldn't be greater than Elijah; but would be destined to do more in the kingdom.

All mentors—*spiritual parents*—should desire that their children would do more, go farther, and reach higher than we have. If not, there's a problem. Hands that are constantly reaching for "more things" aren't destined for greatness, but hands that have the anointing definitely are. According to their spiritual legacy, these hands are destined by God to do *greater works*.

The story of Elijah and Elisha serves as the background for the preparation of prophets in these last days. Their story expresses that people with a prophet's anointing on their lives need to be fully trained in the gift, the call, and the office by someone who is committed to the role of spiritual mentor—a mature person who can discern the workings of the Spirit in the protégé's life, as well as his or her weaknesses.

> **Both "teacher" and "student" could be made whole, because both were affected in the gestation and birthing process.**

The truth is, both the mentor and the one being mentored should be accountable to someone who can challenge them in "comfortable" areas. Elijah and Elisha's relationship was balanced, much like my relationship with Juanita, because we were under my husband's spiritual authority. Therefore, God was able to bring healing and completion in their relationship.

130

Both "teacher" and "student" could be made whole, because both were affected in the gestation and birthing process. Juanita and I came through this process…and because of this, a spiritual legacy has been birthed that will impact generations to come.

Reflection and Study

1)   Do you see similarities between your relationship with your son or daughter in the Spirit and that of Elijah and Elisha? In what ways?

2)   Looking at Elijah, do you see any of his struggles or personality traits operating in you? From reading their story, identify how you can deal with these areas.

3)   Recount an experience with God during this birthing process where He gave you "meat" that sustained you supernaturally for a season that followed.

4)   Have you required your protégé to become "dogmatic" in following after God's mantle upon your life? How?

5)   Remember the four stages to receiving a spiritual inheritance: Gilgal, Bethel, Jericho, and Jordan. Now write a brief "snapshot" outlining each step of your "baby's" journey to destiny.

6)   When your child receives a "double-portion" from you, what will he or she obtain?

7)   Do you see the spirit of Elisha resting upon your spiritual son or daughter? In what ways? Write them down as a memorial unto God.

To the Prophet-in-the-Making

Are you pursuing your spiritual legacy by living in total
submission unto God and to your spiritual mentor?
Do you expect to receive a double-portion
from God for your obedience?
Read Isaiah 40:3–41:2

A Final Word

I have planted, Apollos watered; but God gave the increase…
neither is he that *planteth any thing, neither he that watereth;*
but God that giveth the increase.
—1 Corinthians 3:6–7

The Call of the Mentor

The one who "plants" is no greater than the one who "waters," because both are needed to make the growth process complete. A spiritual increase cannot come unless both of these principles are at work—because they both represent true mentorship. A mentor can be either a planter or a waterer

> **A mentor can be either a planter or a waterer.**

in the life of a prophet-in-the-making. His or her role must be discerned. I also refer to this as "Apostolic Parenting," and I believe it's one of the greatest calls.

Those whom God entrusts to mentor must truly understand what their purpose is in helping others to fulfill their destinies. If a mentor cannot discern his or her position properly, the results could be fatal. Lack of discernment in this area could cause a premature delivery, or even lifetime damage, to a spiritual son or daughter.

I believe the role of the "planter" can be extremely difficult (I consider myself to be in this category). It's a planter's responsibility to develop the protégé from the raw, fetal stages. The focus is to help the "spiritual baby" to understand who she is meant to become and what God has placed inside of her.

The planter understands how to convince the prophet-to-be of his worth so that he can properly identify with Christ. By seeing himself through God's eyes, he can recognize (deep within) that he has great potential to succeed. The planter understands: God sees all of His children as we are destined to become—perfect and complete in Him. So this mentor's role is to aid the protégé in becoming (in this earthly realm) what already has been birthed in the realm of the Spirit.

As a planter, I have the job of plowing through hard and unbroken ground in the protégé's heart. This soil is often rather stony, dry, and infertile. So I must pour out love, compassion, and empathy upon it as the "baby" shares his or her life story with me. My tears nourish the soil and prepare it to "plant" the seed of faith.

> **As a planter, I have the job of plowing through hard and unbroken ground in the protégé's heart.**

After the earth is moist enough to be "tilled and turned over," I discern the conditions of the heart and also when the time has come to "fertilize" the seed within. Once a seed is planted, there can be no resistance…growth must take place. The seed must be allowed to take root within that individual's heart so the mentor can forge a "connection" at just the right time. Then later, the roots of that tiny seed will become intertwined in the life of the spiritual father or mother.

Within the realm of planting, the process of mentorship can be likened to a gardener that oversees the seeds that have been planted. Many "opposing forces" threaten to strip vital nutrients from the heart of the prophet-in-the-making, only to leave the land barren and infertile. Therefore, the mentor must stand guard over the "seeds of greatness" to cultivate, protect, nurture, and prune in the appropriate season.

Once the time for success has arrived and the "planter's" job is complete, the previously immature protégé can move into the place where he or she can be watered. At this point, the second half of the mentoring process must take place. The "waterer" should take over the process.

> **Once the time for success has arrived, the previously immature protégé can move into the place where he or she can be watered.**

Let me pause to say that love is the key to mentorship—whether planting or watering. A spiritual mentor's (i.e., parent's) love, though sometimes difficult to see or understand, is what propels and drives the son or daughter onward to deeper spiritual development. This mentor knows there's a short time available to prepare that person for completion. He or she knows the protégé has a certain amount of time to reach an assigned destination.

It's important, then, that the "son" or "daughter" possesses a servant's heart—because a servant's heart is open. When a "servant" submits to a mentor, then the mentor can easily pour out, release, and share everything that's necessary. Like

> **Whether planting or watering, love is what propels and drives the son or daughter onward to deeper spiritual development.**

Elisha was unto Elijah, the prophet-to-be must display pure humility with no inside tracks or secret agendas. The connection must be sure, because the mentor will be carrying the protégé during that season of development in his or her "spiritual womb."

Personal feelings can warp the process. In all honesty, a mentor doesn't have to be likeable all the time. In fact, there may be instances in the parent-child relationship where mixed emotions or genuine dislike occurs regarding certain elements of the mentor's personality (or vice versa). Rebellion, however, is never an option.

> **Spiritual sons and daughters should never strive against the times and purposes of God during incubation.**

Spiritual sons and daughters should never strive against the times and purposes of God during incubation. It's detrimental to their health and welfare in the Spirit.

Rebellion, especially on the part of the prophet-to-be, will eliminate his or her chances of receiving a rightful inheritance—spiritual "mantles" and other deposits in the Spirit. Remember, rebellion is as the sin of witchcraft. It tries to silence the voice of God when He's speaking into a person's life.

A true mentor has been anointed to impart and release mantles over the lives of his or her spiritual children. The impartation of these mantles come during specific seasons in the mentor's life—times of spiritual transition when the mentor is moving into new levels and/or dimensions, or into new places in ministry. Often, this is referred to as the time of "shifting." Therefore, if each

> **A true mentor imparts and releases "mantles" over the lives of his or her spiritual children.**

person's role in the relationship isn't maintained under the proper perspective, the opportunity for mantle transference may be lost.

Before a promised mantle can be given, the protégé is also responsible to pray for his or her mentor so the true purpose or level to be attained isn't lost. Because the nature of this relationship is highly sensitive, both parties must be careful to stay prayerful, consistently standing in the gap on behalf of one another. The protégé must also be extra careful to ward off any negative or destructive voices, either naturally or spiritually.

Let me close with this. A mentor must always remain cognizant of the fact that he or she isn't expected to be perfect. Trying to put on this façade will ultimately lead a child into pain and disillusionment, because a perfect person can never be weak. This sets up a false standard by which your son or daughter will also measure you. And once a mistake occurs, your baby will lose respect, because he or she expected to be carried by a "perfect parent" all the way through to divine completion. It's much better to be real and "down to earth," and walk humbly before God and man.

In these last days, true mentors are vitally needed.

In these last days, true mentors are vitally needed. So they must be prepared to answer the kingdom call of "parenting" leaders for the next generation. *Who will guide God's anointed vessels through the "furnace of affliction"? Who will walk these prophets-to-be through the refining process so they can emerge as pure gold?* A father...a mother...someone who has been anointed to nurture and sustain an embryonic gift until it is birthed into completion.

The spirit of Elijah (the spirit of mentorship and parenting) is returning to the earth, restoring family unity. And by the unction of God, fathers (in both the natural

A generation is waiting to rise into destiny.

and spiritual realms) are reconnecting with their children. Why do we need anointed mentors to release the prophetic voice? The answer is simple. A generation is waiting to rise into destiny.

To schedule a speaking engagement, or to receive information about other teaching materials and products by Prophetess Veter Nichols, please contact:

Destiny Ministries

P.O. Box 610337

Port Huron, MI 48061–0337

1.810.982.4673 Office

1.810.982.0254 Fax

www.veternichols.com

Upcoming Book Releases – October 2005!

Seven Steps to Front Line Success
Dr. Juanita Bynum

Faithful in Another Man's Work
Dr. Tonya Hall

www.flowpublications.com